Dr. David Ajeigbe

HOW DO YOU FIGHT YOUR BATTLE?!!!

Copyright © 2024 by Dr. David Ajeigbe

All rights reserved. No part of this publication may be reproduced, distributed, or transmitted in any form or by any means, including photocopying, recording, or other electronic or mechanical methods, without the prior written permission of the author, except in the case of brief quotations embodied in critical reviews and certain other noncommercial uses permitted by copyright law.

ISBN: 979-8-89216-042-1 (Paperback)
        979-8-89216-043-8 (Hardback)

Library of Congress Control Number: 2024920925

BookmarcAlliance
California, USA
www.bookmarcalliance.com

Introduction

Some battles are self-imposed while others occur as a matter of being human. It is easier to start wars than to end them. It is easier to begin a war than to initiate a ceasefire. Human battles take different forms. There is no human being without any form of battle or the other. Some samples of battles could be monetary, relationships, health issues, daily needs, feelings of belongings, acceptance or rejection, love or hate, employment or lack of employment, meeting daily needs or inability to meet daily needs, richness or poverty, arrogance, or humility, caring or lack of caring, merciful or merciless, hopefulness or hopelessness, and various other battles. It appears that the battles humans face are multi-faceted. With various types of battles, how could humans win? When humans try to solve those battles by themselves, in their own power they get frustrated, in many cases, and give up. Some humans would engage in activities which instead of resolving their battles drag them down deep into sores battles. "The righteous cry out, and the Lord hears and rescues them from all their troubles. The Lord is near to the brokenhearted and saves those who are crushed in spirit." (Psalm 34:17–18).

When humans call on the Lord, they are to be sure that He would hear their calling and do for them according to His will. Talking about the will of God might appear to be a cop-out until one hears the words of God as pronounced by Peter. "The Lord is not slow about His promise, as some count slowness, but is patient toward you, not willing for any to perish, but for all to come to repentance." (2 Peter 3:9). What God requires of humans is for them to repent of their sins, call on Him, to win whatever type of battle they endure. Although it might appear that the relief from God is coming slowly or the doubt that it will ever coming at all, but humans need to keep their hopes in God because He will, eventually, breakthrough for them. Regardless of where humans are in the plight of their battles God is always aware of them. God's ears are always attentive to the cries of His children. "…for if we live, we live for the Lord, or if we die, we die for the Lord; therefore, whether we live or die, we are the Lord's." (Romans 14:8).

However, at times, God may choose to deliver humans out of dangerous situations by leading humans into His eternal arms. Although, that solution might not appear to be the greatest solution or deliverance that humans would want or expect, but He knows best and does what is best for humans. When we are brokenhearted, he hears our cry and stands with us. When we are crushed and feel overwhelmed, He is there to hold us up. He's ready to listen as you cry out to Him, pleading for His help and for His deliverance. That deliverance may not always come the way we expect, but it will always be for our good (Rom. 8:28). However, God always holds humans in His hands regardless of what the end results of human battles. That is one of the reasons why Paul stated that humans belong to God regardless of whether they are living or dead, as long as they get God involved in their battles they are always save in His hands. The Psalmist testified to this fact by saying;

"One who dwells in the shelter of the Most High"

Will lodge in the shadow of the Almighty.
I will say to the Lord, My refuge and my fortress,
My God, in whom I trust!
For it is He who rescues you from the net of the trapper
And from the deadly plague.
He will cover you with His pinions,
And under His wings you may take refuge;
is faithfulness is a shield and wall.
You will not be afraid of the terror by night,

Or of the arrow that flies by day;
Of the plague that stalks in darkness,
Or of the destruction that devastates at noon.
A thousand may fall at your side
And ten thousand at your right hand,
But it shall not approach you.
You will only look on with your eyes
And see the retaliation against the wicked.
For you have made the Lord, my refuge,
The Most High, your dwelling place.
No evil will happen to you,
Nor will any plague come near your [c]tent.
For He will give His angels orders concerning you,
To protect you in all your ways.
On their hands they will lift you up,

"So that you do not strike your foot against a stone." (Psalm 91:1–12). The sayings by the Psalmist draw humans away from cynicism of the age and focus them back unto God regardless of their varying battles. When people are uncertain about what would happen and how their battles could be resolved, the Psalmist's message is to remind them of the caring providence of God. At a time when humans seem to live only for the moment the Psalmist call is to refocus their confidence back to God who will never leave them as long as they make Him their resting place. God's promise is that, as long as, humans call upon Him, He would answer them, He would be with them, honor them, rescue them from their battles (troubles), and save them. Therefore, humans should move to God with sincerity of hearts and abandon all those things which could serve as hinderances to their close relationship with God.

Are You Seeking the Lord In Your Battles?

Therefore, humans should seek the Lord and make the Lord their Shepherd and conclude like the Psalmist that the Lord is their Shepherd.

"The LORD, The Psalmist's Shepherd."

Psalm of David.
"The LORD is my shepherd,
 I shall not want.
He makes me lie down in green pastures;
He leads me beside quiet waters.
He restores my soul;
He guides me in the paths of righteousness
For His name's sake.
Even though I walk through the valley of the shadow of death,
I fear no evil, for You are with me;
Your rod and Your staff, they comfort me.
You prepare a table before me in the presence of my enemies;
You have anointed my head with oil;
My cup overflows.

Surely goodness and lovingkindness will follow me all the days of my life,
And I will dwell in the house of the LORD forever." (Psalm 23).

According to the Psalmist, there are varieties of human needs which God provides for humans every day. In acknowledging God's provisions, the Psalmist enumerates important human needs. In Maslows' Hierarchy of Needs Theory, he assigned levels to humans needs based on their importance to human existence and achievements. Maslows' hierarchy is in line with the proclamations of the Psalmist.

The physiological needs are the most important human needs which the Psalmist acknowledges that God provides for humans when he said, 'You prepare a table before me,' ... My cup overflows. indicating the provision of food for humans to eat and water to drink. God does the feeding openly for the enemies to see without being able to prevent it and that gives humans the psychological needs they desire. God provides shelter for humans in the reference that God leads humans beside quiet waters which is an indication that God provides peace of mind to humans. The second level of

God's provision for humans is aligned with the Psalmist in regard to resources and security - He restores my soul; He guides me in the paths of righteousness For His name's sake. Even though I walk through the valley of the shadow of death, I fear no evil, for You are with me; Your rod and Your staff, they comfort me I fear no evil, for You are with me. This is an indication that humans should be confident of God's protection for them, always. Humans should be confident in God that He would restore them regardless of their failings as they look up to Him. Therefore, they should regain their self-esteem. The last level of Maslow's hierarchy of needs aligned with the Psalmist saying that 'Surely goodness and lovingkindness will follow me all the days of my life. Humans should know that God will never abandon them in their battles and struggles. They could be rest assured that God is in the business of assisting humans to overcome their battle regardless of how small or how big those battles are.

The battle faced by one individual is different for another individual, however whatever battle a person is facing requires the power and determination to fight it. Humans should be patient while fighting battles because fighting any battle requires focusing, tenacity, patience, and relying on God Who is able. Patience is necessary because one may not be able to lift one thousand pounds at one time, but one can lift one pound one thousand times. It is also said that eating an elephant takes a small bite at a time, although it might take several years to complete the consumption of the elephant, with persistence it could be done. When humans are facing battles, they need to give themselves grace as God as given them and to be patient and to hold to God firmly for their anchor. "…And looking at *them*, Jesus said to them, with people this is impossible, but with God all things are possible." (Matthew 19:26).

The statement by Jesus is applicable to all issues and the battles humans face, they are impossible for humans to win those battles, but winning those battles are only possible with God, therefore, in any circumstance, humans should rely on God.

"… Though times it seems"

Like I'm coming undone
This walk can often feel lonely
No matter what until this race is won
I will stand my ground where hope can be found
I will stand my ground where hope can be found

… Oh, O'Lord O'Lord I know You hear my cry
Your love is lifting me above all the lies
No matter what I face this I know in time
You'll take all that is wrong and make it right
You'll take all that is wrong and make it right

… Your strength is found
At the end of my road
Your grace it reaches to the hurting
Still through the tears and the questioning why
I will stand my ground where hope can be found
I will stand my ground where hope can be found

… Oh, O'Lord O'Lord I know You hear my cry
Your love is lifting me above all the lies
No matter what I face This I know in time
You'll take all that is wrong and make it right
You'll take all that is wrong and make it right
(Right, so right)
Make it right
(Right, so right)
Make it right, right

… I will stand my ground
I will stand my ground

… I will stand my ground where hope can be found
I will stand my ground where hope can be found

… Oh! O'Lord O'Lord I know You hear my cry
Your love is lifting me above all the lies

No matter what I face this I know in time
You'll take all that is wrong and make it right
(take all what is wrong)
You'll take all that is wrong and make it right
(Right, so right)
Make it right
(Right, so right)
Make it right, right"
(Joe Williams/Paul Mabury).

Humans do not possess adequate power within themselves to adequately face and fight the battles they encounter every day of their life. Throughout human existence there is one battle or the other to fight. Everyone's battle might be similar or different from another person's battle, but each person has to devise a means to fight his or her own battle. Those who believe in God and those who do not believe in God all have battles to fight daily. Since having battle is a common trait to humans, no one is immuned from facing one battle or the other, however, how individual fights the battle is important. Life is hard and the burdens humans have to bear could be so tough to bear by themselves. However, humans need to know that God sees their struggles, hardships, and battles, therefore, humans should not bear them all alone because they have a redeemer who is on the standby to handle all their issues successfully.

The Psalmist admonishes humans to cast their burdens upon the Lord. "Cast your burden upon the Lord and He will sustain you;" (Psalm 55:22, NASB). In these pieces of advice, the Psalmist encourages humas to cast their burden on the Lord. Humans are not to worry about their burdens, but to hand them all to the Lord. The only responsibility on the human side is to hand over their burdens to the Lord who knows and who has all the resources of heaven to handle them successfully. He will never allow the righteous to be shaken. When humans go to God with their heavy burdens and with their raging battles, the Lord could replace their heavy burdens with His lighter burden and he could take over their raging battles and set them free. This statement is not a wishful thinking, but it is based on the promise of Christ, the Lord. "Come to Me, all who are weary and burdened, and I will give you rest. Take My yoke upon you and learn from Me, for I am gentle and humble in heart, and YOU WILL FIND REST FOR YOUR SOULS. For My yoke is comfortable, and My burden is light." (Matthew 11:28–30,).

When humans are tired of carrying those burdens and when they are tired of fighting those battles on their own and failing, all that Jesus requires of them is to go to Him for solutions to all their problems.

What Could You Do on Your Own Power?

Fighting your battle by submitting to God is the only winning formular for humans. Jesus said that He is the vine and humans are the branches. He encourages humans to abide in Him. Jesus stated clearly that it is by abiding in Him that humans could be fruitful. It is only by abiding in Jesus that humans could become conquerors. It is only by abiding in Christ that humans could be victorious. He then said that without abiding in Him, humans could do nothing. Therefore, in fighting their battles, humans need to abide in Christ in order to be victorious over those battles regardless of how hard such battles appear to be. "I am the vine, you are the branches; the one who remains in Me, and I in him bears much fruit, for apart from Me you can do nothing. If anyone does not remain in Me, he is thrown away like a branch and dries up; and they gather them and throw them into the fire, and they are burned. If you remain in Me, and My words remain in you, ask whatever you wish, and it will be done for you." (John 15:5–7). When humans are in Christ, Christ will dwell in them and whatever they ask in His name, according to His will, will be done for them. In this saying of Jesus, He gave responsibilities to humans, first, to recognize Him as the vine, the source of their survival, sustenance, and strength, second, humans are to abide in Him, they cannot separate themselves from Him and still expect to receive sustenance from Him. However, if they do separate themselves from Him, they will never be victorious over their battles in the true sense of victory. Their battles will overwhelm them and destroy them, third, Jesus wanted humans to ask him of anything they need, according to His will and it shall be done for them. But, for humans to fight and be victorious over their battles they need to acknowledge God as their Lord and everything else will fall in place for them. Then they can go to the throne of God with boldness and make their petitions known to Him. "How, then, can they call on the one they have not believed in? Romans 10:14…). In order to call on the Lord for assistance in fighting their battles they need to believe in Him. Joel also spoke similar words earlier in the gospel when he said "And it will come about that whoever calls on the name of the LORD Will be delivered… (Joel 2:32). Therefore, in fighting their battles and receiving victories, humans need to believe He who said that He is all powerful and that He is able to resolve their problems and win their battles. They need to acknowledge that they need Him every hour because He is able.

> "Seek the LORD while He may be found; Call upon Him while He is near. Let the wicked abandon his way, And the unrighteous person his thoughts; And let him return to the LORD, And He will have compassion on him, And to our God, For He will abundantly pardon." (Isaiah 55:5–7).

It is important that humans seek the Lord in all their ways when things are good and when things are not so good, in times of prosperity and in times of scarcity, during the time of battles and during the time of victory. Christians should not take on the personality of men. The pride of many men would make them miss their way instead of asking for direction. Before the invention of the Global Positioning System (GPS), it was not uncommon for men to get lost rather than asking for directions. However, women were better at asking for directions and they did not use to get as easily lost as men did. Another aspect of humans is not reading directions on how to put together the things they have just bought and needed to carefully follow directions to put them together as intended by the manufacturer. Men, especially, would lay the direction aside and trust their abilities to put it together, even when it is their first time of putting the object together. Things would appear to be going well until the last piece does not fit in place. It was at that point, in frustration, that the individual would go back to read the manual. At that point some parts of the object might have been damaged or disfigured because the screws had gone into the wrong part of the object. Human tendency is to act like the scenarios above in dealing with God. Instead of going to God for assistance they rely on their own understanding. When humans rely on their own understanding instead of taking it to God, they are not able to win their battles successfully. Since God does not hold grudge against anyone He would come to their aid whenever they ask of Him. However, during their delay in consulting with God they might suffered unnecessarily and carry unneeded burdens. Human should trust God enough and take their battles to Him instead of being blinded by pride. They need to surrender and let Him know that they need Him every hour. The lyric of the song below shows the need for God.

    Lord, I Need You

    Lord I come, I confess
    Bowing here, I find my rest
    Without You, I fall apart
    You're the one that guides my heart.

    … Lord, I need You, oh, I need You
    Every hour, I need
    You My one defense, my righteousness
    Oh God, how I need You.

    … Where sin runs deep, your grace is more
    Where grace is found is where You are
    And where You are, Lord, I am free
    Holiness is Christ in me

> ... Lord, I need You, oh, I need You
> Every hour, I need You
> My one defense, my righteousness
> Oh God, how I need You.
>
> ... So teach my song to rise to You
> When temptation comes my way
> And when I cannot stand, I'll fall on You
> Jesus, You're my hope and stay
>
> ... Lord, I need You, oh, I need You
> Every hour, I need You
> My one defense, my righteousness
> Oh God, how I need You
> You're my one defense, my righteousness
> Oh God, how I need You.
>
> ... My one defense, my righteousness
> Oh God, how I need You." (Matt Maher).

There is no amount of preparation which humans could make without the blessing of the Lord that could be successful, without the blessing of the Lord they are all in vain. The battle belongs to the Lord.

> The battle is the Lord.
> In heavenly armor we'll enter the land
> The battle belongs to the Lord
> No weapon that's fashioned against us shall stand
> The battle belongs to the Lord
>
> We sing glory, honor
> Power and strength to the Lord
> We sing glory, honor
> Power and strength to the Lord.
>
> When the power of darkness comes in like a flood
> The battle belongs to the Lord

He's raised up a standard, the power of His blood
The battle belongs to the Lord.

And we sing glory, honor
Power and strength to the lord
We sing glory, honor
Power and strength to the lord
And we sing glory, honor
Power and strength to the Lord
And we sing glory, honor
Power and strength to the Lord. (Maranatha).

"The horse is prepared for the day of battle, But the victory belongs to the Lord." (Proverbs 21:31). The wall of Jericho fell because the Lord fought the battle for the Israelites.

"Now Jericho was tightly shut because of the sons of Israel; no one went out and no one came in. But the LORD said to Joshua, see, I have handed Jericho over to you, with its king and the valiant warriors. And you shall march around the city, all the men of war circling the city once. You shall do so for six days. Also, seven priests shall carry seven trumpets of rams' horns in front of the ark; then on the seventh day you shall march around the city seven times, and the priests shall blow the trumpets. It shall be that when they make a long blast with the ram's horn, and when you hear the sound of the trumpet, all the people shall shout with a great shout; and the wall of the city will fall down flat, and the people shall go up, everyone straight ahead. So, Joshua, the son of Nun, called the priests and said to them, take up the ark of the covenant, and have seven priests carry seven trumpets of rams' horns in front of the ark of the LORD. Then he said to the people, go forward and march around the city, and the armed men shall go on ahead of the ark of the LORD. And it was so, that when Joshua had spoken to the people, the seven priests carrying the seven trumpets of rams' horns before the LORD went forward and blew the trumpets; and the ark of the covenant of the LORD followed them. And the armed men went ahead of the priests who blew the trumpets, and the rear guard came after the ark, while they continued to blow the trumpets. But Joshua commanded the people, saying, you shall not shout nor let your voice be heard, nor let a word proceed from your mouth, until the day I tell you, 'Shout!' Then you shall shout! So, he had the ark of the Lord taken around the city, circling it once; then they came into the camp and spent the night in the camp. Now Joshua got up early in the morning, and the priests took up the ark of the Lord. Then the seven priests carrying the seven trumpets of rams' horns in front of the ark of the Lord went on continually and blew the trumpets; and the armed men went ahead of them, and the rear guard came after the ark of the Lord, while they continued to blow the trumpets. So, the second day they marched around the city once and returned to the camp; they did the same for six days. Then on the seventh day they got up early at the dawning of the day and marched around the city in the same way seven times; only on that day did they march around the city seven times. And at the seventh time, when the priests blew the trumpets, Joshua said to the people, Shout! For the Lord has given you the city. But the city shall be designated for destruction, it and everything that is in it belongs to the Lord; only Rahab the prostitute and all who are with her in the house shall live, because she hid the messengers whom we sent. But as for you, only keep yourselves from the things designated for destruction, so that you do not covet them and take some of the designated things and turn the camp of Israel into something designated for destruction and bring disaster on it. But all the silver and gold, and articles of bronze and iron are holy to the Lord; they shall go into the treasury of the Lord. So, the people shouted, and the priests blew the trumpets; and when the people heard the sound of the trumpet, the people shouted with a great shout, and the wall fell down flat, so that the people went up into the city, everyone straight ahead, and they took the city. They utterly destroyed everything in the city, both man and woman, young and old, and ox, sheep, and donkey, with the edge of the sword. And Joshua said to the two men who had spied out the land, go into the prostitute's house and bring the woman and all she has out of there, just as you have sworn to her. So, the young men who were spies went in and brought out Rahab, her father, her mother, her brothers, and all she had; they also brought out all her relatives and placed them outside the camp of Israel. Then they burned the city with fire, and all that was in it. Only the silver and gold, and the articles of bronze and iron, they put into the treasury of the house of the LORD. However, Rahab the prostitute and her father's household and all she had, Joshua spared; and she has lived in the midst of Israel to this day, because she hid the messengers whom Joshua sent to spy out Jericho. Then Joshua made them take an oath at that time, saying, cursed before the Lord is the man who rises up and builds this city of Jericho; with the loss of his firstborn, he will lay its foundation, and with the loss of his youngest son he will set up its gates. So, the LORD was with Joshua, and his fame was in all the land." (Joshua 6:1–27). When fighting battles, it is important to rely on God for directions and guidance and more importantly to follow as God directs. The Israelites relied on God and followed His directions. Here are the steps God directed the Israelites to take in their battle against Jericho. The priests blew the horns in front of the Ark of the Covenant,

How Do You Fight Your Battle?!!!

The Israelites marched once a day for the first six days, on the seventh day the Israelites marched seven times around the city of

and the Israelites went in and conquered the city. Throughout their dealings in the battle of Jericho the Israelites listened and carried out the instructions from God. As a result of the obedience of the Israelites to God's instruction they were victorious over their enemies. Therefore, it is important for humans to trust and obey God in order to win their battles because God knows best. God told the Israelites that He had conquered their enemies for them, they trusted, and obeyed Him.

Dr. David Ajeigbe

"When we walk with the Lord in the light of His Word"

What a glory He sheds on our way!
While we do His good will, He abides with us still
And with all who will trust and obey
Trust and obey, for there's no other way
To be happy in Jesus, but to trust and obey.
Not a shadow can rise, not a cloud in the skies
But His smile quickly drives it away
Not a doubt or a fear, not a sigh or a tear
Can abide while we trust and obey.

Oh, Trust and obey, for there's no other way
To be happy in Jesus, but to trust and obey.
Then in fellowship sweet we will sit at His feet
Or we'll walk by His side in the way
What He says we will do, where He sends, we will go
Never fear, only trust, and obey.

Trust and obey, for there's no other way
To be happy in Jesus, but to trust and obey.

Oh, Trust and obey, for there's no other way
To be happy in Jesus, but to trust and obey.

And 'Tis so sweet to trust in Jesus
Just to take Him at His Word
Just to rest upon His promise
Just to know, thus saith the Lord."

Jesus, Jesus, how I trust Him!
How I've proved Him o'er and o'er
Jesus, Jesus, precious Jesus!
Oh, for grace to trust Him more.

Lord oh, for grace to trust You more."
(Barry Collecutt).

    The battle belongs to God and He is the only one Who could successfully fight human battles, but all He expects of humans is to trust and obey Him. The Israelites could have been afraid, but because of their trust in God they were not afraid and they came out victoriously at the end of their ordeal.

David and Goliath - are you David and is your battle Goliath – how do you fight them and how could you win?

"Now the Philistines gathered their armies for battle; and they were gathered at Socoh which belongs to Judah, and they camped between Socoh and Azekah, in Ephes-dammim. Saul and the men of Israel were assembled and camped in the Valley of Elah, and they drew up in battle formation to confront the Philistines.... Then a champion came forward from the army encampment of the Philistines, named Goliath, from Gath. His height was six cubits and a span. And he had a bronze helmet on his head, and he wore scale-armor which weighed five thousand shekels of bronze. He also had bronze greaves on his legs and a bronze saber slung between his shoulders. The shaft of his spear was like a weaver's beam, and the head of his spear weighed six hundred shekels of iron; and his shield-carrier walked in front of him. He stood and shouted to the ranks of Israel and said to them, why do you come out to draw up in battle formation? Am I not the Philistine, and you the servants of Saul? Choose a man as your representative and have him come down to me. If he is able to fight me and kill me, then we will become your servants; but if I prevail against him and kill him, then you shall become our servants and serve us. Then the Philistine said, I have defied the ranks of Israel this day! Give me a man, so that we may fight together. When Saul and all Israel heard these words of the Philistine, they were dismayed and very fearful. Now, David was the son of the Ephrathite of Bethlehem in Judah, the man whose name was Jesse, and he had eight sons.... So, David was the youngest.... And the Philistine came forward morning and evening and took his stand for forty days. Then, Jesse said to his son David, take now for your brothers an ephah of this roasted grain and these ten loaves, and run to the camp to your brothers. Bring also these ten slices of cheese to the commander of their thousand and look into the well-being of your brothers and bring back confirmation from them.... So, David got up early in the morning and left the flock with a keeper and took the supplies and went as Jesse had commanded him....Israel and the Philistines drew up in battle formation, army against army. Then David left the baggage in the care of the baggage keeper and ran to the battle line. And he entered and greeted his brothers. As he was speaking with them, behold, the champion, the Philistine from Gath named Goliath, was coming up from the army of the Philistines, and he spoke these same words; and David heard him. When all the men of Israel saw the man, they fled from him and were very fearful. And the men of Israel said, have you seen this man who is coming up? Surely, he is coming up to defy Israel. And it will be that the king will make the man who kills him wealthy with great riches and will give him his daughter and make his father's house free in Israel. Then David said to the men who were standing by him, what will be done for the man who kills this Philistine and rids Israel of the disgrace? For who is this uncircumcised Philistine, that he has dared to defy the armies of the living God? The people answered him in agreement with this statement, saying, this is what will be done for the man who kills him. Now Eliab his oldest brother heard him when he spoke to the men; and Eliab's anger burned against David and he said, why is it that you have come down? And with whom have you left those few sheep in the wilderness? I myself know your insolence and the wickedness of your heart; for you have come down in order to see the battle. But David said, what have I done now? Was it not just a question? Then he turned away from him to another and said the same thing; and the people replied with the same words as before.... When the words that David spoke were heard, they informed Saul, and he sent for him. And David said to Saul, May no one's heart fail on account of him; your servant will go and fight this Philistine! But Saul said to David, you are not able to go against this Philistine to fight him; for you are only a youth, while he has been a warrior since his youth. But David said to Saul, your servant was tending his father's sheep. When a lion or a bear came and took a sheep from the flock, I went out after it and attacked it, and rescued the sheep from its mouth; and when it rose up against me, I grabbed it by its mane and struck it and killed it. Your servant has killed both the lion and the bear; and this uncircumcised Philistine will be like one of them, since he has defied the armies of the living God. And David said, "The Lord who saved me from the paw of the lion and the paw of the bear, He will save me from the hand of this Philistine. So, Saul said to David, go, and may the Lord be with you. Then Saul clothed David with his military attire and put a bronze helmet on his head and outfitted him with armor. And David strapped his sword over his military attire and struggled at walking, for he had not trained with the armor. So, David said to Saul, I cannot go with these, because I have not trained with them. And David took them off. Then he took his staff in his hand and chose for himself five smooth stones from the brook and put them in the shepherd's bag which he had, that is, in his shepherd's pouch, and his sling was in his hand; and he approached the Philistine. Then the Philistine came and approached David, with the shield-bearer in front of him. When the Philistine looked and saw David, he was contemptuous of him; for he was only a youth, and reddish, with a handsome appearance. So, the Philistine said to David, am I a dog, that you come to me with sticks? And the Philistine cursed David by his gods. The Philistine also said to David, come to me, and I will give your flesh to the birds of the sky and the wild animals. But David said to the Philistine, you come to me with a sword, a spear, and a saber, but I come to you in the name of the Lord of armies, the God of the armies of Israel, whom you have defied. This day the Lord will hand you over to me, and I will strike you and remove your head from you. Then I will give the dead bodies of the army of the Philistines this day to the birds of the sky and the wild animals of the earth, so that all the earth may know that there is a God in Israel, and that this entire assembly may know that the Lord does not save by sword or by spear; for the battle is the Lord's, and He will hand you over to us! Then it happened, when the Philistine came closer to meet David, that David ran quickly toward the battle line to meet the Philistine. And David put his hand into his bag and took from it, a stone and slung it and struck the Philistine on his forehead. And the stone penetrated his forehead, and he fell on his face to the ground. So, David prevailed over the Philistine with the sling and the stone: he struck the Philistine and killed him, and there was no sword in David's hand. Then David ran and stood over the Philistine and took his sword and drew it out of its sheath and finished him and cut off his head with it. When the Philistines saw that their champion was dead, they fled. Then the men of Israel and Judah rose up and shouted, and they pursued the Philistines as far as the valley, and to the gates of Ekron. And the Philistine dead lay along the way to Shaaraim, even to Gath and Ekron. Then the sons of Israel returned from their close pursuit of the Philistines and plundered their camps. And David took the Philistine's head and brought it to Jerusalem, but he put his weapons in his tent." (1 Samuel 17:1–54). The Philistines and the Israelites were set for battle. Goliath, the champion of the Philistine's army was an experienced warrior who had been fighting battles since his youth. He was skilled in preparing and carrying out battle plans. He was an expert in gauging the strength of his enemies and in preserving his army resources. He was good at estimating the number of his soldiers needed to fight any particular battle. His stature (height and build) was towering over his enemies. He truly was a scary human being in his appearance. For the battle with the Israelites, he prepared extra well in all kinds of ammunition of war and with all kinds of protective gear at the time. He decided to single handedly fight the battle against a chosen representative of the Israelites army on a one-to-one combat with him. He looked down on the Israelites and their army and he considered them inferior to the Philistines' army.

The Israelites were afraid and scared of the towering figure of Goliath and of all his ammunition to fight and the protective gear on him. No one in the Israelites army dared to step out to challenge and fight with Goliath. Goliath was so emboldened that he challenged the Israelites daily and continuously for about forty days or more. Goliath became very cocky and dismissive of the Israelites and their army. He badgered and harassed them daily. Goliath relied on his expertise and the strength of the Philistine army. However, God worked in mysterious ways when humans think that they have got to the end of the road with no opportunity to return, it is at those times that God showed up, and performs His miracles in ways not expected, and from the source not anticipated. At the time when the Israelites' grown-up soldiers were cringing because of the fear of Goliath, David showed up, but he was a small boy and he enquired of what was going on after observing the fears in the faces of the Israelites' soldiers. His brothers were not happy with him for showing up where he should not have shown up, as a lad. Upon hearing what was going on and observing the countenances on the faces of Israelites, David was moved to action and he decided to volunteer to have a hand-to-hand combat with Goliath, the giant, and the champion of the Philistine army. Saul, the Israelites' king did his best to dissuade David, but David was determined to go and fight Goliath. David recounted how God had helped him battle lions and bears as a shepherd boy whenever those animals took his sheep. He was not only able to protect his sheep, but he was able to kill those animals with God's assistance. At that point Saul wanted to provide some protection for David by having him wear his military attire and by putting a bronze helmet on his head and outfitted him with armor with his sword strapped over his military attire. However, David being a young lad in the war outfit meant for an adult found them too big and too heavy for him. The armor became a burden and a hinderance to him so that it weighed him down to the point that he was going to be unable to function. David decided to trust God for his protection instead of human protection. Therefore, he shed off all human armor and protective gear and he put on the armor of God. He then prayed to God for His protection instead of relying on human protection. David believed that the Lord would fight the battle for him. Therefore, David's trust in God increased and he prayed to God for vindication of the Israelites and for the vindication of God's own name by giving him victory over the giant. As the battle was set, Goliath looked down on the small lad – David, and he felt insulted that the Israelites sent a small boy to fight him, a giant, in a one-to-one battle. Goliath felt so insulted that he promised and boasted that he would give the flesh of the boy (David) to the birds of the air for a snack. However, David, the young boy, told Goliath that God would give Goliath to him in victory and that he would kill him (Goliath) because the battle belongs to the Lord. David trusted in God and he was able to kill Goliath with the sling shot of a stone.

He cut the head of Goliath with Goliath's own sword. This occurrence poured 'cold water' in the hearts of the Philistine army, and they fled. The Israelites bravery was rekindled and they pursued and conquered the Philistines. Every human being has a goliath. Do you know your goliath? Any issue(s), problem(s), or situation(s) is/are your giant(s). Those goliaths come in different forms, in different ways, and it could be overwhelming dealing with those giants by one's own power, but by the power of God everything is possible.

"David killed Goliath though it seemed impossible

Who'd have thought a single stone could make a giant fall
'Cause He was just a kid and by comparison was small
But held within the hands of God, He was invincible.

So, this I will remember when the battle comes to me
To fix my eyes on things above and not on what I see
So in the deepest struggle, in the face of great defeat
My unfair advantage is that Jesus stands with me.

And all it ever takes
Is a little seed of faith
Big enough to bring down every giant
I don't have to be afraid
In the hands of God, I'm brave
He's training me to bring down every giant
So I will overcome my Goliath
I will overcome my Goliath.

Courage comes from knowing that I'm walking with the Lord
No matter what I face, I know that He has gone before
This will be the battle cry that hell cannot ignore
Jesus is the Risen One, He's overcome it all.

All it ever takes
Is a little seed of faith
Big enough to bring down every giant
I don't have to be afraid
In the hands of God, I'm brave
He's training me to bring down every giant
So I will overcome my Goliath
I will overcome my Goliath.

Rise up, for the battle is the Lord's
Rise up, for the battle is the Lord's
Rise up, for the battle is the Lord's
Rise up, for the battle is the Lord's
Rise up, for the battle is the Lord's
Rise up, for the battle is the Lord's

And all it ever takes
Is a little seed of faith
Big enough to bring down every giant
I don't have to be afraid
In the hands of God, I'm brave
He's training me to bring down every giant
And I will overcome my Goliath
I will overcome my Goliath
I will overcome my Goliath
I will overcome my Goliath."
(Mitch Wong/Lucy Naomi Grimble).

Jesus' disciples were unable to cure a boy who was demon possessed and they were so ashamed that they approached Jesus privately to ask why they failed. "Then the disciples came to Jesus privately and said, Why could we not cast it out? And He said to them, Because of your meager faith; for truly I say to you, if you have faith the size of a mustard seed, you will say to this mountain, 'Move from here to there,' and it will move; and nothing will be impossible for you" (Matthew 17:19–21). Humans do not have enough resources or adequacy to face their goliaths, however, with faith and reliance on God who is able and reliable, humans could overcome and become conquerors over those goliaths as they raise their heads. "He shall say, Hear, Israel: Today you are going into battle against your enemies. Do not be faint-hearted, or afraid, do not panic or be terrified by them. For the Lord your God is the one who goes with you to fight for you against your enemies to give you victory" (Deuteronomy 20:1–4). Whenever humans want to fight their battles on their own power they could be guaranteed to fail in most cases because human efforts are not adequate enough, but a lift from God would always give them victory over whatever battle they are fighting. This was made vivid in the healing of the paralyzed man at the pool. "After these things there was a feast of the Jews, and Jesus went up to Jerusalem. Now in Jerusalem, by the Sheep Gate, there is a pool which in Hebrew is called Bethesda, having five porticoes. In these porticoes lay a multitude of those who were sick, blind, limping, or paralyzed. Now a man was there who had been ill for thirty-eight years. Jesus, upon seeing this man lying there and knowing that he had already been in that condition for a long time, said to him, do you want to get well? The sick man answered Him, Sir, I have no man to put me into the pool when the water is stirred up, but while I am coming, another steps down before me. Jesus said to him, get up, pick up your pallet and walk. Immediately, the man became well, and picked up his pallet and began to walk. Now it was a Sabbath on that day. So, the Jews were saying to the man who was cured, it is a Sabbath, and it is not permissible for you to carry your pallet. But he answered them, He who made me well was the one who said to me, pick up your pallet and walk. They asked him, who is the man who said to you, 'pick it up and walk? But the man who was healed did not know who it was, for Jesus had slipped away while there was a crowd in that place. Afterward, Jesus found him in the temple and said to him, behold, you have become well; do not sin anymore, so that nothing worse happens to you. The man went away, and informed the Jews that it was Jesus who had made him well. For this reason, the Jews were persecuting Jesus because He was doing these things on a Sabbath. But He answered them, My Father is working until now, and I Myself am working." (John 5:1–17). In this healing, the paralyzed man had been fighting his battle in the best way he knew how to fight it, but to no avail. He was not able, he was powerless, and his efforts year after year always ended in failures. Despite several failures which he had faced he never gave up; he was persistent in his efforts. Every opportunity which presented itself to him ended up in disappointment because other people who were in need, as he was, always took advantage of his handicap and took the opportunity away from him. Despite his disappointment, he kept going back every time for about thirty-eight years. How long have you been dealing with your battles and disappointments? How long will you continue to fight your battles by yourself when there is a sure source of strength to fight and win your battles? God is patiently waiting for you to reach out to Him to fight and win your battles. How long will you hold back from asking Him to fight your battles? The passage above did not say how the paralyzed man has been able to get to the pool to receive relieve from his battle, but his hope and persistence was remarkable. The paralyzed man never gave up. Humans should be persistent when praying to God to overcome their battles when their battles still persist. Even though the paralyzed man has been fighting his battle alone for a long time when Jesus came around to assist him fight his battle, he readily followed Jesus' directive. The paralyzed man listened to Jesus and Jesus was able to fight and win his battle of many years instantaneously. The paralyzed man achieved what he had been longing for over many years at the twinkle of an eye when Jesus showed up. Ask Jesus to show up in your life to fight your battles and all will be well, immediately. You are not strong enough to fight your own battle successfully, therefore, submit yourself to Him who is able. After Jesus had settled the paralyzed man's battle, there came some detractors who were trying to take away the joy the paralyzed man experienced. When he was suffering in his battle none of them offered to assist him to get into the pool to get healed on any day of the week, however when he was relieved of his battle, they were attempting to put him in another bondage to reduce his joy. This should be a lesson for humans that not everyone is joyous when God has overcome their battles. They need not be concerned about such responses from others, but they are to point them to God who has assisted them to win their battles. This response from others should give an individual opportunity to give their testimony of what God has done for them just as the paralyzed man did. It is said that there is no testimony without a test. The paralyzed man's test (his paralysis) gave him the opportunity to give his testimony to his accusers.

The lyrics of the song below show the love of God for sinners. Because of Christ's sacrifice of His life, humans have abundant life and their sins were/are forgiven. This is not because of their goodness it is a gift to humans from God.

When humans have doubts about their security, God assures their security. When humans are buried under the weight of their sins the grace of God uncovers them. When humans are unable to lift up their head high to God, God stoops down, holds them up, looks into their eyes, and declares them His own.

"I am guilty

Ashamed of what I've done, what I've become
These <u>hands</u> are dirty
I dare not lift them up to the Holy one
You <u>plead</u> my cause

You right my wrongs
You <u>break</u> my chains.
You overcome.
You gave Your life.
To give me mine
You say that I am free.
How can it be?

How can it be?
I've been hiding.
Afraid I've let you down, <u>inside</u> I doubt.
That You <u>still</u> love me
But in Your eyes, there's only <u>grace</u> now.
You <u>plead</u> my cause.
You <u>right</u> my wrongs
You <u>break</u> my chains.
You overcome.
You gave Your life.
To give me mine
You say that I am free.
How can it be?
How can it be?
Though I fall, You can make me new
From this <u>death</u> I will rise with You
Oh the <u>grace</u> reaching out for me.
How can it be?
How can it be?
You <u>plead</u> my cause.
You <u>right</u> my wrongs
You <u>break</u> my chains.
You overcome.
You gave Your life.
To give me mine
You say that I am free.
You <u>plead</u> my cause.
You <u>right</u> my wrongs
You <u>break</u> my chains.
You overcome.
You gave Your life.
To give me mine
You say that I am free.
How can it be?
How can it be. (Lauren Daigle).

The Bible states that: "For while we were still helpless, at the right time Christ died for the ungodly." (Romans 5:6). The Bible states that at the right time Jesus came and gave perpetual saving grace to sinners by dying for them. Jesus hands are not short and His timing is not late in rescuing humans, but He was/is prompt, and He came timely to save sinners. Christ saved/saves sinners when they had/have come to the end of the road and thought/think that there was no hope for them, Jesus gave them hope.

When humans think that they do not worth anything, Jesus demonstrated that they are worth His life. At the time when humans were/are ready to give up on fighting their battles Jesus took over their battles and made/make them overcomers. Humans should reach out to God when they feel that they are struggling alone and to realize that they are not alone in their battles, but that God is very near to them. Their prayers should include the opportunity to share God's presence with other people. They are to pray that their test will give them opportunities to witness to others of God's grace which is sufficient for them. Therefore, whatever battle you are fighting take them to Jesus who is able to overcome for you. Jesus is ready to set you free from the bondage of sin just as the Bible says: "Jesus answered them, truly, truly I say to you, everyone who commits sin is a slave of sin. Now the slave does not remain in the house forever; the son does remain forever. So, if the Son sets you free, you really will be free." (John 8:34–36). When humans are going through various types of battles, they may be asking 'why?' There might be no easy answers for human struggles, however, humans should picture the situation of Jesus praying while His disciples were struggling with sleep. Although Jesus was not at their presence, He had them in His mind. Humans should feel encouraged when they feel alone that God is ever present with them. Humans need to know that God will not abandon them in their battles, but He will find a way for them to win when they feel that the battles are too strong for them. When humans are fearful of the battles ahead of them, they should know that God is with them, in their corner, in power, in love, and that He will never abandon them.

"… I need the kinda love that can outlast the night

I need the kinda love that is willing to fight

… When the going gets tough
And my strength's not enough
I see You showing up like never before
This battle for my heart
You took on from the start
You are the peace when my mind's at war
And oh

… You will never stop fighting for me
When I can't fight for myself
Every word is a promise You keep
'Cause You love me like nobody else
You stand up for me in the darkest night
When my faith is weak You're still by my side
You will never stop fighting for me
You will never stop fighting for me

… In the perfect timing You make all things right
You paint a silver lining in this heart of mine

… When the going gets tough
And my strength's not enough

How Do You Fight Your Battle?!!!

I see You showing up like never before
This battle for my heart
You took on from the start
You are the peace when my mind's at war
And oh

… You will never stop fighting for me
When I can't fight for myself
Every word is a promise You keep
'Cause You love me like nobody else
You stand up for me in the darkest night
When my faith is weak You're still by my side
You will never stop fighting for me
You will never stop fighting for me

… Your love
Is winning me over
Your heart
Is pulling me closer
Your love
Is winning me over
Your heart
Is pulling me closer

… You will never stop
Fighting for me, fighting for me
Every word is a promise You keep
Ohh, yeah

… You will never stop fighting for me
When I can't fight for myself (when I can't)
Every word is a promise You keep (ohh)
'Cause You love me like nobody else
You stand up for me in the darkest night (You stand up for me in the dark)
When my faith is weak You're still by my side (yeah, yeah, my side)
You will never stop fighting for me
You will never stop fighting for me."
(Ethan Hulse/Jordan Sapp/Riley Clemons)

Jesus came to the world to live with humans in order to partake of their experiences. Jesus extends His love and power to all and nothing can separate humans from His love for them. Jesus sees battles which humans are fighting through the lens of His spirit, and He is interceding for humans before God. "Who is the one who condemns? Christ Jesus is He who died, but rather, was raised, who is at the right hand of God, who also intercedes for us." (Romans 8:34). "My little children, I am writing these things to you so that you may not sin. And if anyone sins, we have an Advocate with the Father, Jesus Christ the righteous;" (1 John 2:1). "Therefore, He is also able to save forever those who come to God through Him, since He always lives to make intercession for them." (Hebrews 7:25). Whenever humans get into any kind of earthly trouble, they seek reputable lawyers to represent them before a judge with the hope that those lawyers will be able to plead their case in order to free them from the consequences of the law(s) they have violated. Getting such great lawyers is not cheap, some people spend so much money to the extent of losing their possessions, fortunes, and reputations. After all their efforts, those lawyers might not be able to save them from the consequences of their violation of human laws, they might still face the consequences which go along with their violations. However, in the case of Jesus He represents humans before God as the greatest successful lawyer. Jesus, as the greatest attorney gives His service for free without any string attached. Jesus is the only attorney in the world who does not charge for His service, but paid the cost of representing humans with His blood and life. In that case, Christ's representation of humans before God does not cost humans anything but it is a free gift from Jesus for His service to humans. Humans are to confirm that, although salvation is free to them, however, they should remember that forgiving human sins are not that free because it cost Jesus His life. It was a high price for Jesus to set humans free. Salvation is not something for which humans can pay or for which they deserve by way of good works, it is the gift of God. "For the wages of sin is death, but the gracious gift of God is eternal life in Christ Jesus our Lord." (Romans 6:23). "But the gracious gift is not like the offense. For if by the offense of the one the many died, much more did the grace of God and the gift by the grace of the one Man, Jesus Christ, overflow to the many. The gift is not like that which came through the one who sinned; for on the one hand the judgment arose from one offense, resulting in condemnation, but on the other hand the gracious gift arose from many offenses, resulting in justification. For if by the offense of the one, death reigned through the one, much more will those who receive the abundance of grace and of the gift of righteousness reign in life through the One, Jesus Christ. So then, as through one offense the result was condemnation to all mankind, so also through one act of righteousness the result was justification of life to all mankind." (Romans 5:15–8). Further, Paul expressed in Ephesians that it was by grace that they were saved through faith and that was not of themselves: it is the gift of God: "For by grace you have been saved through faith; and this is not of yourselves, it is the gift of God." (Ephesians 2:8). Peter told Simon that the gift of God cannot be purchased with money (Acts 8:20). When humans have done all that God expects of them, they still are unable to earn what God has promised them. Naaman, the leper, did as prophet Elisha commanded him by dipping himself into the Jordan River seven times, he did not earn the cleansing of his leprosy, but God gave it to him as a free gift. (2 Kings 5:10–14). The salvation of human soul is not cheap, but it is extremely expensive in the form of the blood and the sacrificial death of Christ which cannot be measured inform of gold, silver, or any kind of monetary currency. If humans are saved with gold, silver, or any kind of monetary currency, the values of those assets are not stable, but fluctuate from time to time and their purchasing powers are neither stable nor reliable. But the purchasing power of Jesus is free, stable, and reliable at all times, therefore the purchasing power of Jesus 'blood and His death are able to fight any sin-battle with which humans are engaged at any time. Gold and silver are corruptible commodities which could not redeem corruptible human beings just as the precious blood of Jesus could because He was/is without spot and without blemish. "Knowing that you were not redeemed with perishable things like silver or gold from your futile way of life inherited from your forefathers, but with precious blood, as of a lamb unblemished and spotless, the blood of Christ." (I Peter 1:18–19). "But God demonstrates His own love toward us, in that while we were still sinners, Christ died for us." (Romans 5:8). No gift has ever been as great as the gift of eternal life given to humans by God. Although the gift from God to humans is free, however, there are some responsibilities which humans have to practice in order to be worthy of the gift of eternal life. One of the responsibilities for humans is to submit to the authority of Christ, the great physician. "And having been perfected, He became the source of eternal salvation for all those who obey Him." (Hebrews 5:9). Another responsibility for humans is to obey Christ of what He has commanded humans. A protocol for the way to behave was outlined by Jesus in the statement above. In any organization, family, or in relations there is always protocol on how to do things or how to represent the organization or the family. In similar manner Jesus has protocol for humans, especially for those who have accepted His free gift, to obey Him. "Having been buried with Him in baptism, in which you were also raised with Him through faith in the working of God, who raised Him from the dead. And when you were dead in your wrongdoings and the uncircumcision of your flesh, He made you alive together with Him, having forgiven us all our wrongdoings," (Colossians 2:12–13). After God has won human battles, He gave them the responsibility to walk in newness of life. "Therefore, we have been buried with Him through baptism into death, so that, just as Christ was raised from the dead through the glory of the Father, so we too may walk in newness of life. (Romans 6:4). After being buried with Christ and being raised with Him humans are to refrain from participating in the immoral worldly desires of the flesh. "Do not love the world nor the things in the world. If anyone loves the world, the love of the Father is not in him. For all that is in the world, the lust of the flesh and the lust of the eyes and the boastful pride of life, is not from the Father, but is from the world. (1 John 2:15–6). Choosing rather to endure ill-treatment with the people of God than to enjoy the temporary pleasures of sin, (Hebrews 11:25). Humans are to give up the pleasure of sin. Being followers of God should cost humans something as a sacrifice for the Lord who has sacrificed all, including His life in order to fight their battles and give them freedom. Jesus taught about counting the cost when He said, "For which one of you, when he wants to build a tower, does not first sit down and calculate the cost, to see if he has enough to complete *it*? Otherwise, when he has laid a foundation and is not able to finish, all who are watching it will begin to ridicule him, saying, 'This person began to build, and was not able to finish!' Or what king, when he sets out to meet another king in battle, will not first sit down and consider whether he is strong enough with ten thousand men to face the one coming against him with twenty thousand? Otherwise, while the other is still far away, he sends a delegation and requests terms of peace. (Luke 14:2, 8–32. In the two examples above, Jesus was admonishing his followers and all human beings not to bring disgrace to themselves and ridicules to the name of the Lord. He expects humans to have a solid plan before embarking on any project. Jesus said, "Whoever does not carry his own cross and come after Me cannot be My disciple.... So then, none of you can be My disciple who does not give up all his own possessions." (Luke 14:27, 33). When humans follow God and do His will, they may face some persecution with their friends and family members. Those persecutions might cause divisions and hatred within the family or friends. The descensions caused could be so big that it creates battles withing the family and friends. Having such dissension is not comfortable and the hardships it creates could be so overwhelming to individuals to the point that they might go back from doing the will of God. Jesus was aware that such could happen, and He was preparing His followers to be prepared to give Him priority over the battle because he could overcome for them. "Indeed, all who want to live in a godly way in Christ Jesus will be persecuted." (II Timothy 3:12). Although salvation is free, it is not cheap! The Father, the Son, and the Holy Spirit have paid for it through their own sacrifices. However, every human being is to make his or her own decision to give all that is needed to partake in the sacrifice accompanying it. Although Jesus has provided salvation to all, it will not be valuable to humans unless humans claim it. God does not force His redemption on humans, but He gives humans the freedom to accept the salvation which He has provided.

The salvation provided could be likened to the availability of banks all around humans. The benefits of using the bank for safekeeping of money is obvious, however no one forces anyone to put their money in the bank where it is safe and where it could grow. Some people decide to keep their money in their house or in any other unsafe locations where it does not grow and where it is open to theft. Jesus provided salvation for people and He offers it to all without cohesions, but accepting Him is voluntary. He did not force anyone to accept Him, but He wished that all will come to His saving grace. "For the grace of God has appeared, bringing salvation to all people, instructing us to deny ungodliness and worldly desires and to live sensibly, righteously, and in a godly manner in the present age, looking for the blessed hope and the appearing of the glory of our great God and Savior, Christ Jesus, who gave Himself for us to redeem us from every lawless deed, and to purify for Himself a people for His own possession, eager for good deeds." (Titus 2:11–14). Jesus has completed the work of salvation and He has made it available to all, the responsibility to take advantage of the salvation which God has provided is left to humans to take advantage of. Human battles have been won by God, but humans should avail themselves the opportunity to follow and accept God's victory.

Fighting the Battle of Anger and Revenge

Anger and revenge are some natural corrosive intense emotional evils to relationships.

Those emotions could befall humans. They are like plagues which could infect humans very easily. Those rash intense emotions could easily sneak on humans when they least expect them. They could easily take over human responses to others in ways which are not edifying to the Lord. Angry impulses are never satisfying to those who succumb to them, but leave individuals with feelings of guilt afterwards. Anger generally does not bring about any good outcome, but ends in unplanned adverse effects. Therefore, before humans succumb to anger, they should pause and examine the source of their anger. If humans know the trigger for their anger, they might be able to guide against such outburst of anger by letting go of them and surrendering them to God. Human anger cannot contribute to bringing about the goodness of God and His gospel to those who need them. "You know this, my beloved brothers and sisters. Now everyone must be quick to hear, slow to speak, and slow to anger; for a man's anger does not bring about the righteousness of God." (James 1:19–20). James admonished all his hearers to be quick in hearing what is being said by someone else and ponder over it before responding and to be slow to be angry. This caution is important because by responding hastily, especially in anger, it could bring regret and damage to relationships. Anger does not only bring damage to relationships with people, but it could demean the goodness of God before others. Therefore, humans are admonished to be patient with anger and shift every emotion through the lens that God would want humans to handle them. The steadfast love of God quenches every thirst of contention. Anger could lead to isolation from others, especially, from those with whom the individual is angry. Anger could break relationships, destroy communications, break apart joy, and destroy the personal health of those who participate in regular angry outbursts.

Being slow to anger is a great principle of a balanced life as Solomon described it. "One who is slow to anger is better than the mighty, and one who rules his spirit, than one who captures a city." (Proverbs 16:32). Solomon made clear in his discourse that nothing is as valuable as being slow to anger. Any achievement humans could attain rank behind being well-tempered (slow to anger). Being slow to anger is a virtue which God expects humans to possess and to put into practice daily in dealings with the circumstances of life. It is human to be angry, but to be controlled by anger is the great sin that God warned humans against. The Bible warned humans in these verses; "Do not be eager in your spirit to be angry, for anger resides in the heart of fools." (Ecclesiastes 7:9). "If the ruler's temper rises against you, do not abandon your place, because composure puts great offenses to rest. "(Ecclesiastes 10:4). "All bitterness, wrath, anger, clamor, and slander must be removed from you, along with all malice." (Ephesians 4:31)." Therefore, I want the men in every place to pray, lifting up holy hands, without anger and dispute." (1 Timothy 2:8). "Turn from evil and do good; Seek peace and pursue it." (Psalm 34:14). The Bible verses above remind humans and direct them on how to handle their natural tendencies to explode in anger. God expects humans to act in wisdom, but acting quickly in anger is a sign of foolishness in which God does not want humans to be engaged. Although anger could be justified in certain instances, holding on to anger could eventually hurt individuals. Moses rightly broke the covenant tablets at the horrible adultery of the people. Meekness is not shy to correct what is wrong; rather, it is bold. When Moses met with the Lord to receive the law, the Israelites strayed away and began worshiping idol instead of God who rescued them from slavery. Moses, in anger, rightly broke the law-tablets at the ungrateful adultery of the Israelites. Correcting the wrongs done, in meekness, is a sign of strength and boldness. Moses' anger was a sign of disappointment at the ungratefulness of the people of Israel. Moses was angry because he realized what the Israelites were about to lose. He could not imagine how short the Israelites' memory could be of the salvation God provided them from their bondage. Moses' love for the Israelites produced his anger towards their lack of appreciation and going back to their vomit. "Like a dog that returns to its vomit, so is a fool who repeats his foolishness." (Proverbs 26:11). Moses saw the action of the Israelites to be laced with foolishness and he was angry. Just as a dog returning to its vomit, the Israelites were clamoring to return to bondage. Moses expected the Israelites to know better, but when they demonstrated that they did not, despite all that the Lord had done for them, he became very disappointed and angry. However, when God was about to destroy them, Moses stood between the Israelites and God's anger. Moses courageously interceded for the Israelites and saved them from the impending wrath of God. Meekness renounces power and refrains from using power as the world does. Since God wants all good things for humans, He does not want the evils associated with anger to overtake them. There is a saying regarding constant holding to anger, that it is like holding on to hot coals. Your anger may burn hot and bright, but in the end, you're the one getting burned. Anger could lead to bitterness and bitterness could destroy humans. Anybody can become angry, that is easy, but to be angry with the right person and to the right degree and at the right time and for the right purpose, and in the right way - that is not within everybody's power and it is not easy. (Aristotle). When humans are accustomed to anger it is difficult to discard those impulses, however, by submitting to God, everything is possible. Self-control plays a vital role in managing the expression of anger. Human anger could easily turn to unbridled rage and it could easily spiral out of control into revenge. God is cognizant of the evils of uncontrolled anger and for those reasons He commanded humans to stay away from uncontrolled anger and to allow Him to control their emotions. "Cease from anger and abandon wrath; Do not get upset; it leads only to evildoing. For evildoers will be eliminated, but those who wait for the Lord, they will inherit the land." (Psalm 37:8–9). "But the fruit of the Spirit is love, joy, peace, patience, kindness, goodness, faithfulness, gentleness, self-control; against such things there is no law." (Galatians 5:22–23). "For God has not given us a spirit of timidity, but of power and love and discipline." (2 Timothy 1:7). In every aspect of life, self-discipline is an asset which is a valuable ingredient to human existence and happiness. There is nothing tangible, of value, lasting, and rewarding achieved by humans without one form of self-discipline or the other. "Be angry, and yet do not sin; do not let the sun go down on your anger," (Ephesians 4:26). In this admonition by Paul, he realized that every human being could be angry, especially when there is any wrong done, however, he wanted the anger to be temporary and for humans not to be consumed by them. Cain was consumed by his anger against his brother and his uncontrolled anger led him to kill his brother, Abel. "Cain, the firstborn, was a farmer, and his brother Abel was a shepherd. The brothers made sacrifices to God, but God favored Abel's sacrifice instead of Cain's. Cain then murdered Abel, where upon God punished Cain by condemning him to a life of wandering." (https://en.wikipedia.org › wiki › Cain_and_A).

There were some orders or hierarchies on who could enter certain sections of the temple. The temple was divided into sections with allocations of which group or individuals who could enter certain locations. "The Israelites could enter the court of the Gentiles only; the priests could serve in the Holy Place; the high priest alone could enter the Holy of Holies but once a year—on the Day of Atonement." (S.v. "tabernacle," 15:6, 8, 7.)

Although the temple is a holy place, not a place to trade, do regular business, or exchange money, however, this idea became corrupted, and people were allowed to perform business and trading. In essence some people were going to the temple not to worship God, but to carry out their various business activities including money changing, selling, and buying sacrificial animals and birds. The purpose of the temple became adulterated by the greediness of the people charging money for the people who went there. The Court of the Gentiles was the outer court that surrounded the inner sacred courts (Utley, Beloved Disciple, 27; Grassmick, "Mark," 157). It became allowed practice to use the Court of the Gentiles for all sorts of trading and money changing to occur. Thousands of Jews made pilgrimages to Jerusalem for various religious feasts and observations. During those times, authorities allowed money changers and animal sellers inside the outer court of the temple. The people had to change the Roman currency to the acceptable currency by the traders. Instead of doing the willing and dealing outside the temple courts it was allowed inside the Courts of the Gentiles. This practice deprived the Gentiles the full use of the only area of access to them to concentrate with one mind in worshiping God because of all the trading commotions going on around them as they tried to worship God. The Court of the Gentiles was sacred for the Gentiles to worship God, but it was profaned by the traders for financial profit. Observing what was going on, the turning of a place to worship God into a marketplace was not pleasing to Jesus. The temple and any part of it was meant to be used for the worship of God and not for any form of financial transactions, therefore, when the temple or any part of it was not being used for its intended purpose, Jesus was not happy at that practice. Jesus was determined to put a dramatic end to the misuse of God's house as the house of merchandise. Jesus got angry; however, it was not a selfish anger as humans display. The merchants were making it hard for common people to worship God. The outer court was full of bleating lambs and sellers hawking their wares and people exchanging money. No one was focused on God. When humans get together to worship God, they must put aside all distractions and personal agendas. Jesus wants humans to experience the joy and peace without outside distractions in devotion to Him. The practice of using the Court of the Gentiles for merchandising appeared to be prejudicial because it was happening only in the section assigned to the minority group, the Gentiles. Jesus wanted everyone's attention to be focused on God regardless of their ethnicity. Jesus wanted all the people present to be able to have uninterrupted opportunities to worship God. The tables set and the trading materials being used appeared to be hinderances to fully worshipping God and that was not pleasing to Christ. Therefore, He was determined to clean the Court of the Gentiles by turning over the objects of hinderances to worshipping God with undivided minds. Jesus was unhappy or angry about the actions of the people and not with the people. Jesus in His anger was able to separate the people form their actions which He attacked. "And Jesus entered the temple area and drove out all those who were selling and buying on the temple grounds, and He overturned the tables of the money changers and the seats of those who were selling doves. And He said to them, "It is written: MY HOUSE WILL BE CALLED A HOUSE OF PRAYER'; but you are making it a den of robbers." (Matthew 21:12–13).

Anger, at times, could get out of control if humans are not on the watch out for it. It is important to let go of issues or individuals who could bring about human anger. It is easy to fall into the temptation of taking revenge against those who have offended or angered humans. However, when humans take it on themselves to take revenge on others, they are taking the role of God. Therefore, humans should refrain from taking over the role of God by taken revenge. God is the true avenger of all evils, but humans are not adequate to take the role of God. "Do not say, "I will repay evil"; Wait for the LORD, and He will save you." (Proverbs 20:22). "Never take your own revenge, beloved, but leave room for the wrath *of God*, for it is written: "VENGEANCE IS MINE, I WILL REPAY," says the Lord." Romans 12:19). Whenever humans dwell on the wrong done to them by other human beings they could become enraged and want to 'get even' by avenging them. The best Christian response is to let go and forgive the wrong done when humans forgive others, they will get forgiveness from God. "But if you do not forgive other people, then your Father will not forgive your offenses." (Matthew 6:15). Only God is perfect, but no human being is perfect or qualified to judge and dole out punishments in form of revenge on other humans. Humans should let go of the wrong done to them by others instead of taking revenge. Humans should show the love of God to all regardless of what wrong others have done them. Humans are to examine their priorities and tendencies to partake in anger and revenge, confess, reject them, and surrender them to God in order to have peace with themselves and with others. "Do not make friends with a person given to anger, or go with a hot-tempered person, or you will learn his ways and find a snare for yourself." (Proverbs 22:24–25). Humans are to be mindful with whom they associate themselves. "Do not be deceived: Bad company corrupts good morals. Sober up morally and stop sinning, for some have no knowledge of God. I say this to your shame. " (1 Corinthians 15:33–34). If humans associate themselves with people who are prone to anger, they might become like them. However, if Christians show good examples on how they handle situations which provoke them to anger, they could be witnesses to others. This could be a test of their love for God which could be a good example of their endurance which could give them a valuable testimony to those with whom they associate. Their test could become valuable testimony to others and bring them to the saving grace of God. Paul said similar statement: "Whatever you do in word or deed, do everything in the name of the Lord Jesus, giving thanks through Him to God the Father. (Colossians 3:17). At times people in authority feel that they need to show their anger with little things that their subordinates or employees do wrong instead of correcting them humanly. They feel that showing their anger against their subordinates or employees would scare them and prevent them from committing any or similar errors in the future. However, what such expression of anger does to the subordinates or employees is paralyzing them from independent actions which could bring greater and better results for the fear of making mistakes. Therefore, expressed anger which is perceived by the superior to promote creativity and increased productivity has the opposite effect on morality and productivity. People will be more likely to avoid their association with or work for a superior who is full of anger. Regardless of how good humans are at what they do, their reputation could be marred by their angry lifestyle.

Once humans are enslaved to anger their tolerance for patience begins to diminish and they become more and more angry at minor issues. They become experts in the expression of anger and their other beneficial skills begin to atrophy as the level of their anger suffocates them. Anger could give a short time result, but its adverse lasting effects could be irreversible in productivity and to the reputation of the one displaying anger and on those who are recipients of the anger. Some successful people are angry people. Their anger tends to diminish their success and lower their reputation amongst those who know them. Such successful people could appear to be good and well-mannered in public but are like 'junkyard dogs' behind closed doors. It is those who are closer to them who bear the blunt of their anger.

Role of Pride/Boasting/Arrogance in Fighting Battle.

Pride, boasting, and arrogance are in the family of some stumbling blocks preventing humans from being victorious in waging and winning battles. Pride leads to the loss of precious positions that could have belonged to humans. A great example of this concept was the situation with Satan and God. Satan had a great position earlier in the kingdom of God, but he forfeited his position with God because of his pride and jealousy of God. "How you have fallen from heaven, you star of the morning, son of the dawn! You have been cut down to the earth, you who defeated the nations! But you said in your heart, I will ascend to heaven; I will raise my throne above the stars of God, And I will sit on the mount of assembly. In the recesses of the north. I will ascend above the heights of the clouds; I will make myself like the Most High." (Isaiah 12:12–14). Satan was jealous of God and he aspired to be higher than God and because of his pride he was thrown out of heaven. Pride never does anything good for human beings just as it did not do anything good for Satan, but it made him despised by all. Related results await humans leading to their loss of position(s) and inheritance(s) which could have been theirs. Pride leads to the loss of relationships with other humans and with God. The easiest and fastest way to lose in battles is through practice and expression of pride. "Everyone who is proud in heart is an abomination to the

Lord; be assured, he will not go unpunished. Pride goes before destruction, a haughty spirit before a fall." (Proverbs 16:5, 18). God is not out to hurt your pride He is out to kill your pride." (Reena). Pride is sin because it looks down on others and it neither puts the value of other human beings into consideration nor does it recognize God as provider of all good things. "But as it is, you boast in your arrogance; all such boasting is evil." (James 4:16). The personalities of prideful people include insecurity, boasting, controlling, self-righteousness, judgmental attitude, power hungry, perfectionist, people-pleasing, ungrateful, and rebellious. Those characteristics are abominable to the Lord. Those characteristics are ingredients for humans to lose their battles. Humans with pride do not recognize God's saving power, the provisions that humans do get because of God's grace and not by any good that humans have done. Whatever humans achieve is through the grace of God and it is not through the goodness they have done, therefore, they have no merit to boast about any goodness they have received because it is only by the grace of God. "For by grace, you have been saved through faith; and his is not of yourselves, it is the gift of God; not a result of works, so that no one may boast." (Ephesians 2:8–9). When humans boast and get prideful about what God has done for them, they behave as if they achieve them on their own power without giving glory to God. "For who considers you as superior? What do you have that you did not receive? And if you did receive it, why do you boast as if you had not received it?" (1 Corinthians 4:7). When humans behave pridefully, they are being ungrateful to God, which is sin. How does pride keep us from God? Pride, in particular, gives humans the false illusion that they do not need God. David writes: "In his pride the wicked man does not seek Him; in all his thoughts there is no room for God" (Psalm 10:4). Those with pride do not seek or have room for God in their lives and their deliberations. Proud people put themselves above everything or everybody else. They felt that everything should surround them and whatever they say should be final without consideration for anyone else's position or input. Just as the second letter in 'SIN' is I, so is their belief that only their word or opinion should rule the day. Each of their statements starts or ends with 'I.'

They are so self-conceited that they refuse to take pieces of advice which could help them in fighting their battle(s), Even when it is obvious to them that they have done wrong they refuse to say sorry and they refuse to take responsibilities for their wrongdoing. They perceive admitting wrong and asking for forgiveness as signs of weakness, therefore, they never take responsibility. By not taking responsibility they forfeit getting useful opinions from others which could assist them in fighting their battles. Those who could provide them with useful assistance withhold the assistance and allow the proud to wallow in their battles. The story was told of a father who was very proudful and would not apologize to anyone when the wrong he had done was very obvious. He never apologized to his spouse, or to his children, or even to his friends. One day he wrongly disciplined one of his children, which he and everyone else present, including the child, quickly recognized that he was wrong in the discipline. It would have been better immediately when he recognized his error to approach the child and apologize but he neither admitted his error nor apologized to his child. If he had apologized to the child as soon as he realized his error, he would have been held in high esteem by his child. But because he refused and played down his error, he lost the respect of his child, and he ruined their relationship. People who do not apologize or take responsibility for their actions are losing out on the gains they could earn for their names. They feel that asking for forgiveness or apologizing for the wrong done is a sign of weakness without having the understanding that asking for forgiveness or recognizing their wrong makes them stronger and it earns them the respect of others. God expects humans to recognize their errors and to make right any wrong which they have done to any human being in order for their service to Him to be acceptable. Just as humans might not apologize to other human being so they might not acknowledge their sins to God and ask for forgiveness and such self-righteousness could be in the way of their prayers to God. Instead of seeking God to assist them in fighting their battles they face those battles in their own understanding and do not follow Him in all their ways. When humans have such attitude their trust in God is diminished and their ways become crooked. "Trust in the LORD with all your heart and do not lean on your own understanding. In all your ways acknowledge Him, and He will make your paths straight." Proverbs 3:5–6). In order to be successful in fighting battles, humans need to lean on God, seek His directions, and not rely on their own wisdom or strength, but to trust God who is able. In order to be subjected to God's leading, humans need to abandon pride, boasting, and arrogance. "…So, Solomon finished the house of the Lord and the king's palace, and successfully completed everything that he had planned on doing in the house of the Lord and in his palace. Then the Lord appeared to Solomon at night and said to him, "I have heard your prayer and have chosen this place for Myself as a house of sacrifice. If I shut up the heavens so that there is no rain, or if I command the locust to devour the land, or if I send a plague among My people, and My people who are called by My name humble themselves, and pray and seek My face, and turn from their wicked ways, then I will hear from heaven, and I will forgive their sin and will heal their land. Now, My eyes will be open and My ears attentive to the prayer offered in this place. (2 Chronicles 7:11–16). God promised to bless His people (the Israelite), to hear their prayers, and to forgive their sins. God promised to fight their battles and to give them victory only if they confess their sins, seek His forgiveness, abandon their arrogance, and pride, and pray to Him. When humans acknowledge that they are not of their own, but that they have been bought for a price and thus submit themselves to God, then they will be victorious over their battles. Human battles could be financial, health issues, human relationships, failures, and inability to get ahead, however, when humans rely on God for those various battles which appear to be big mountains, could all be rolled away through the power of God. Relying on God is the only solution to human battles. "Seek the Lord and His strength; Seek His face continually. "(1 Chronicles 16:11). Seeking God is not only when humans have problems but continually even when there appears to be no battles to fight and when things are going well. "The LORD of hosts is with us; the God of Jacob is our stronghold." (Psalm 46:7). The word "stronghold" could be considered a secure place with protective surroundings which could not be breached by enemies. The natural position of such a place makes it very difficult for the enemies to assail. God is depicted by the Psalmist as someone which no enemy could overpower when He is acting as a shield for humans. When humans run under the wing and protection of God all their battles are surmountable, and no enemy could get to them. The presence of God is not temporary, and humans could count on His presence to always be with them in fighting their battles.

"You are, You are always there

You are, You are always there
God, You were always there for me
God, You have always loved me
Sometimes I'm afraid, and sometimes I fall down
But God, You are always there for me
Wrapped in the brightness of Your glory
How could I forget?
Lost in the beauty of Your majesty, God
You stole my heart and brought my eyes to tears
You calmed my storm and silenced all my fears
Sometimes I'm afraid, and sometimes I fall down
But God, You are always there for me
You are always there for me
You are always there for me
You are, You are always there
You are, You are always there
You are always there for me

God, You know all my problems
God, You know all my pain
And every time I'm down, You lift me up
You're reaching out for me
You're reaching out, oh, You're reaching out
Wrapped in the brightness of Your glory
How could I forget?
Lost in the beauty of Your majesty, God

You stole my heart and brought my eyes to tears
You calmed my storm and silenced all my fears
Sometimes I'm afraid, and sometimes I fall down

But God, You are always there for me
You are always there for me
You are always there for me
You are, You are always there
You are, You are always there
You are always there for me
Oh, You are always there
You are always there
Sometimes I'm afraid, and sometimes I fall down, woah
You are always there for me

Woah, always there
You are always there for me
You are, You are always there
You are, You are always there
You are always there for me" (Marshall Marshall).

On their pilgrimage from Egypt, the Israelites faced many difficulties. In their despair God promised to be with them. God told them that His presence will be with them in their difficulties. "And He said, My presence shall go with you, and I will give you rest. Then he said to Him, If Your presence does not go with us, do not lead us up from here." (Exodus 33:14–15). This is an example that God will always be with and guide humans in fighting whatever battles they have and that He would not abandon them in their difficulties. Therefore, humans should have the confidence that God is their refuge. This is why the Psalmist said, "God is our refuge and strength, A very ready help in trouble. Therefore, we will not fear, though the earth shakes and the mountains slip into the heart of the sea; Though its waters roar *and* foam, Though the mountains quake at its swelling pride. "Psalm 46:1–3). The Psalmist was so confident with God's presence and assistance for him to fight his battles that regardless of whatever uproar and upheavals were going on around him, he had confidence in God's saving grace to fight his battles, so he did not waiver. He remained steadfast with the Lord of glory, his redeemer who was always near to him. David was able to fight and win his battles because of his trust in God. Therefore, humans should emulate the character of

David in his trust of God to neither be afraid nor waiver when all around them appear to be falling apart, but to trust God Who is with them will put everything together as new. Humans' sure availability of help from God is just as certain as it was for David in his battle with Goliath.

Sarah was ninety years old when an angel told her and her husband that they would have a son. Sarah was curious and, laughed in disbelief, and asked a logical question: "So Sarah laughed to herself, saying, "After I have become old, am I to have pleasure, my lord being old also?" But the Lord said to Abraham, "Why did Sarah laugh, saying, 'Shall I actually give birth to a child, when I am so old?' Is anything too difficult for the LORD? At the appointed time I will return to you, at this time next year, and Sarah will have a son." (Genesis 18:12–15). The Lord made plain that although both of them were very old it was not beyond His power to make it possible for Sarah to be pregnant and bear a son. God won the battle for Sarah and Abraham and gave them a son, named Isaac, to carry the pivotal Abrahamic covenant to the generations to follow. When humans think that their battles are lost causes, God is ready to make the impossible possible. When humans thought that there is no way, God creates a wide path for them out of their battles. This was the case with Mary, who was a virgin and could not bear a child, however, God spoke through Isaiah that a virgin would bear a child. "Therefore, the Lord Himself will give you a sign: Behold, the virgin will conceive and give birth to a son, and she will name Him Immanuel." (Isaiah 7:14).

When the angel notified Mary, she was very surprised and wondered how it could happen to have a child when she was a virgin, but the angel reassured her that all would be well and she believed. "Greetings favored one! The Lord is with you." But she was very perplexed at this statement and was pondering what kind of greeting this was. And the angel said to her, "Do not be afraid, Mary, for you have found favor with God. And behold, you will conceive in your womb and give birth to a son, and you shall name Him Jesus. He will be great and will be called the Son of the Most High; and the Lord God will give Him the throne of His father David; and He will reign over the house of Jacob forever, and His kingdom will have no end." But Mary said to the angel, "How will this be, since I am a virgin?" The angel answered and said to her, "The Holy Spirit will come upon you, and the power of the Most High will overshadow you; for that reason also the holy Child will be called the Son of God. And behold, even your relative Elizabeth herself has conceived a son in her old age, and she who was called infertile is now in her sixth month. For nothing will be impossible with God." And Mary said, "Behold, the Lord's bondservant; may it be done to me according to your word." "For with God nothing shall be impossible" (Luke 1:28–38). God spoke through the angel and the angel acknowledged the impossibilities of what he had said to Mary for humans, however, the angel reassured Mary that Mary's concern was very minor for God because there is nothing impossible for God to do. In three gospels, the fact that the power of God is not limited is stated clearly by Jesus. "And looking at them, Jesus said to them, "With people this is impossible, but with God all things are possible." (Matthew 19:26). " Looking at them, Jesus said, "With people it is impossible, but not with God; for all things are possible with God." (Mark 10:27). "But He said, "The things that are impossible with people are possible with God." (Luke 18; 27). For humans to reverse the impossible to possibility they need to learn and obey the teachings of God. When God's will has been done, heaven-sent lift will win human battles successfully. Humans should follow basic scriptural themes which are faith, courage, strength, and focus. When humans truthfully adhere to those themes the Lord will make possible all the impossibilities in their lives and God will overcome for them.

Paul sited the exemplary faith of Noah, Abraham, Moses, the wall of Jericho, Abel, Enoch, Sarah, David, Isaac, Jacob, Joseph, Samuel, and Joshua, (Hebrews 11:4–34). Noah had faith in God that when he was warned of the doom coming to the earth, he built an ark in the desert. His faith in God propelled him to have no doubt on what God had revealed to him and he was prepared to save human beings. His faith was nurtured through his knowledge of God. Abraham moved from his familiar land to the land he did not know anything about without a doubt, but with the faith that wherever God led him must be a better place for him.

Abraham was ready to sacrifice his only son of his old age with the understanding and faith that God who gave the only son to him at his old age had a plan for him even though he did not know what the plan was. Abraham obeyed and God blessed him for it. Moses' parent hid him for about three months with the faith that God had something better for him and that God would make a provision for his life. The wall of Jericho fell because the Israelites obeyed and had faith in God. It was only through faith that the Israelites followed the direction which no war planner will embark on, but because the direction came from God, the Israelites had the faith that God knew best and with their faith intact they adhered to God's instructions. Abel had faith in God that God who provided all he had for him would provide more for him as long as he was faithful to God. His faith in God led him to give the best sacrifice to God and God accepted his offering. As a result of his faith God won the battle of death for him. Enoch became victorious over the battle of death. Death did not have power over him because of his faith in God, God took him without experiencing death. Sarah was able to conceive, even beyond *the* proper time in a woman's life to bear a child. David was able to win the battle against Goliath because he realized that he was not powerful by himself to face Goliath, however he had faith in God that He would come to his aide and won the battle against the giant for him. David was not disappointed in his faith in God because the Lord came through for him. Through his faith Isaac blessed Jacob and Esau, regarding things which he envisaged would come to pass. Thought of what to happen in the future, when Jacob was dying, he blessed the sons of Joseph, and he worshiped God despite the fact that his strength was fading away and he had to support himself on the top of his staff. When Joseph also was on his death bed, he had the faith that one day the Israelites would be released from the land of Egypt. Joseph was sure of it that he told the Israelites not to leave his bones behind in Egypt, but to carry his bones with them when the time comes in the future for them to leave Egypt. Samuel had bad news to tell his audience. Giving such bad news to his audience could lead him lose favor with his master. However, he was not afraid, but he delivered God's message boldly to his master with the faith that God would be with him. (1 Samuel 3).

After Joshua took over the leadership of the Israelites after the death of Moses they had an insurmountable task ahead of them, they had to cross the mighty River Jordan. Amidst them were children, women, old and young who might not know how to swim. They also had their animals and belongings to carry across the river. The task became very great for Joshua to handle. However, Joshua did not forget God's assurance to him that He would be with him to lead the people to the promised land. Whenever the spirit of doubt crept in him, he overcame them with his faith in God. River Jordan became a big battle in his life and an obstacle to his leadership, however, he relied on God for help and his faith grew stronger. God solved his battle because of his faith in Him. Joshua overcame the battle of River Jordan and he was able to lead the Israelites through the river unscathed. There are several battles which could burden humans at one time or the other in their lifetimes. Some of the battles humans fight everyday are weariness, heavy heartedness with grief for something precious lost, clouds of sorrow for opportunities missed, anxiety for the future, and the thought of dying. When all those battles are raging and it appears that there is no end in sight the only solid rock to run to for solace is Jesus Christ, the Lord, and Savior Who is the best friend that could not be moved and Who understands human plight because He once suffered like humans do.

> Therefore, take it all to Jesus in prayer.
> Tell it to Jesus
> "Are you weary, are you heavy-hearted?
> Tell it to Jesus,
> Tell it to Jesus;
> Are you grieving over joys departed?
> Tell it to Jesus alone.
>
> > *Refrain:*
> > Tell it to Jesus, tell it to Jesus,
> > He is a friend that's well-known;

You've no other such a friend or brother,
Tell it to Jesus alone.

Do the tears flow down your cheeks unbidden?
Tell it to Jesus,
Tell it to Jesus;
Have you sins that to men's eyes are hidden?
Tell it to Jesus alone.

Do you fear the gath'ring clouds of sorrow?
Tell it to Jesus,
Tell it to Jesus;

Are you anxious what shall be tomorrow?
Tell it to Jesus alone.

Are you troubled at the thought of dying?
Tell it to Jesus,
Tell it to Jesus;
For Christ's coming kingdom are you sighing?
Tell it to Jesus alone." (Edmund S. Lorenz).

"Faithful is He who calls you, and He also will do it." (Thessalonians 5:24). God has called humans to come to Him and put their focus on Him because He is faithful and He will do all that He has promised. Therefore, humans should be rest assured that everything which God has said would come to pass because He keeps His words. "Heaven and earth will pass away, but My words will not pass away." (Matthew 24:35). The earth and heaven are temporary, they are here for a while and they will eventually disappear, however, the words of Jesus are permanent with no variables to them and they will last when everything else has disappeared. Therefore, humans should run to Jesus the solid rock which never moves. Humans could rely on God because He is faithful and He has called them. Humans should listen to the voice of God and yield to His calling in fighting their battles. When battles are testing human resolve, they should realize that those battles are propelling them to maturity and steadfastness.

How Do You Fight Your Battle?!!!

"Consider it all joy, my brothers, and sisters, when you encounter various [trials, knowing that the testing of your faith produces endurance. And let endurance have its perfect result, so that you may be perfect and complete, lacking in nothing." (James 1:2–4). James admonished humans that while they are going through trials and battles as a preparation for their goodness, therefore, they are not to get discouraged or lose heart because of the benefits that would follow the battles or trials. Humans would come out better at the end of the battles or trials than they were before the battles or trials. Human battles or trials could be compared to the process of refining gold. In refining crude gold, it is melted and treated with chloride. This process converts any foreign objects or minerals still remaining in the gold into chloride. Chloride is then carried away from the gold. This refining process for gold produces about 99.5% pure gold. However, when humans are going through their battles and getting God involved in the process, they are 100% purified and are able to win their battles. With God involvement in fighting human battles all impurities, encumbrances, and the weight of sins weighing humans down are completely removed. Humans should put all their focus on God and not get distracted by the battles raging around them. This is not an easy task for humans to tackle because battles are like shining objects which could easily divert one's attention from the real objects. Battles have tendencies to do the same for humans. Distractions make humans

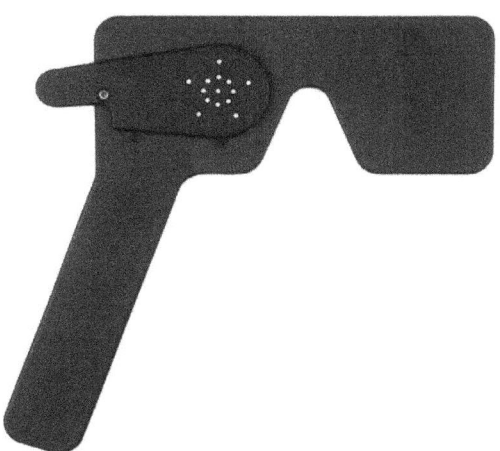

take their eyes away from God and focus on their own solutions which are inferior to the solution which God could provide. It is important for humans to set their eyes on Jesus for when they do, the things of the world will grow small. There is a device in the optometry office called Optical Occluded Eye Device which is used to determine the ability to read letters. It has two parts; one part is to block one eye at a time and leave the other eye to do the recognition of the letters projected across the room. Upon completing that process with one eye, the same device is used but at this point some pinholes on the device are employed to assist in clearly defining each letter as projected. The same process is repeated for the other eye. Looking through the pin holes requires a lot of focus. The focus has to be on a single hole of the several pin holes on the device. It is not easy to maintain such focus because other pinholes serve as shining objects distracting individuals from maintaining focus on one pinhole. These are the problems humans face when there are battles to fight. When human focus is directed to other areas for winning their battles instead of turning to Christ, they are bound to lose. A vivid example of this could be seen with the encounter of Peter with Jesus on the water. "And in the fourth watch of the night He came to them, walking on the sea. When the disciples saw Him walking on the sea, they were terrified, and said, "It is a ghost!" And they cried out in fear. But immediately Jesus spoke to them, saying, "Take courage, it is I; do not be afraid." Peter responded and said to Him, "Lord, if it is You, command me to come to You on the water."And He said, "Come!" And Peter got out of the boat and walked on the water and came toward Jesus. But seeing the wind, he became frightened, and when he began to sink, he cried out, saying, "Lord, save me!" Immediately Jesus reached out with His hand and took hold of him, and said to him, "(You of little faith, why did you doubt?" (Matthew 14:25–31). Peter was confident and trusting of Jesus when Jesus told him to come to Him on the water of the sea, Peter was as light as a feather when he trusted and focused on Jesus, he was able to walk on the water unimpeded by the water or by the waves of the ocean. But, as soon as his focus was distracted by other events around him his trust in Jesus decreased, he became as heavy as a rock with all his fears, his faith waned and he began to sink. However, he immediately realized who his Savior was and he focused his attention back on Jesus. Jesus saved him from his predicament and restored him. "And He went a little beyond them, and fell on His face and prayed, saying, "My Father, if it is possible, let this cup pass from Me; yet not as I will, but as You will." And He came to the disciples and found them sleeping, and He said to Peter, "So, you men could not keep watch with Me for one hour? Keep watching and praying, so that you do not come into temptation; the spirit is willing, but the flesh is weak." (Matthew 26:39–41). In another instance with Peter and other disciples, they failed the expectation of Jesus and He realized that even though humans want to do something in their spirit, but if they succumb to the wish of the flesh, they would be rendered unable to accomplish them. In this case, Jesus was admonishing them to not only 'follow their hearts', but to submit to the spirit of God to lead them.

> "This is what the Lord says:
> "Cursed is the man who trusts in mankind
> And makes flesh his strength,
> And whose heart turns away from the Lord.
> For he will be like a bush in the desert,
> And will not see when prosperity comes,
> But will live in stony wastes in the wilderness,
> A land of salt that is not inhabited.
> Blessed is the man who trusts in the Lord,
> And whose trust is the Lord.
> For he will be like a tree planted by the water
> That extends its roots by a stream,
> And does not fear when the heat comes;
> But its leaves will be green,
> And it will not be anxious in a year of drought,
> Nor cease to yield fruit." (Jeremiah 17:5–8).

The Lord knows and understands human beings for their unreliability; therefore, He warned all not to trust human beings. Humans are not able to resolve their own problems talk less of being able to fight other human beings' battles. Therefore, God warned humans through Jeremiah in the above statements. Instead of assisting in resolving human problems they might be adding to them and instead of providing relief they might intentionally or unintentionally adding to the problems by their pieces of advice or by their lack of action. However, a trust in Christ is assuring, lasting, dependable, and all encompassing.

> Fix Our Eyes on Jesus
> "All of our darkness
> Our fears and frustrations
> Our hurts and our doubts
> Lord, we lay them at your feet
> All of our weakness
> The pull of temptation
> The burden of failure
> We lay these at your feet
>
> Pre Chorus
>
> Help us throw off all that hinders us
> The entanglement of sin
> Let us turn from worldly idols
> Let us run, run to You
>
> Chorus
>
> We fix our eyes on Jesus, our perfect Redeemer
> You're the author of our faith
> You bore the cross, our sin, our shame
> So we fix our eyes on Jesus, our glorious Saviour
> You have overcome the world
> Lord we thank You, and take heart
> All of our longing
> Our greed and our envy
> Our selfish desires
> Lord, we lay them at your feet
> All of our anger
> The wounds of resentiment
> Our slavery to pride
> Lord, we lay these at your feet ." (Kew Baptist).

Strength and Courage are some essential qualities which God expects of humans in fighting their battles. So, Moses went and spoke these words to all Israel. And he said to them, "I am 120 years old today; I am no longer able to go out and come in, and the Lord has told me, 'You shall not cross this Jordan.' It is the Lord your God who is going to cross ahead of you; He Himself will destroy these nations before you, and you shall dispossess them. Joshua is the one who is going to cross ahead of you, just as the Lord has spoken. And the Lord will do to them just as He did to Sihon and Og, the kings of the Amorites, and to their land, when He destroyed them. The Lord will turn them over to you, and you will do to them in accordance with all the commandments which I have commanded you. Be strong and courageous, do not be afraid or in dread of them, for the Lord your God is the One who is going with you. He will not desert you or abandon you." (Deuteronomy 31:1–6). When Moses was very old, he had to transition his leadership to Joshua. Moses did the transition openly, probably for at least two reasons. The first possible reason was because he had been with the Israelites through 'thick and thin' and the Israelites trusted his leadership. When he was not able to lead them more effectively any longer, the Israelites might be wondering what would become of them and their families in the desert. Therefore, he had an open transition to assure the Israelites that they would be in 'good hands.' He wanted them to know that God who had been with him during his leadership would continue to be with them during the leadership of Joshua. He then gave them some pieces of advice to be courageous and neither to be afraid nor to be faint-hearted because the Lord would be with them. For his second reason for an open transition, he delivered God's message to them that they should not be afraid of their enemies because the Lord had won their battles. His open support for Joshua's leadership provided the Israelites the confidence they needed to 'cement' their support of Joshua. Moses' strategy worked; the Israelites threw their support behind Joshua. God also declared his support to him to complete His promise to the Israelites. "No one will be able to oppose you all the days of your life. Just as I have been with Moses, I will be with you; I will not desert you nor abandon you. Be strong and courageous, for you shall give this people possession of the land which I swore to their fathers to give them. Only be strong and very courageous; be careful to do according to all the Law which Moses My servant commanded you; do not turn from it to the right or to the left, so that you may achieve success wherever you go. Have I not commanded you? Be strong and courageous! Do not be terrified nor dismayed, for the Lord your God is with you wherever you go.' Just as we obeyed Moses in all things, so we will obey you; only may the Lord your God be with you as He was with Moses. Anyone who rebels against your command and does not obey your words in all that you command him, shall be put to death; only be strong and courageous." (Joshua 31:5, 7, 9, 17, 18). Joshua then said to them, "Do not fear or be dismayed! Be strong and courageous, for the Lord will do this to all your enemies with whom you fight." (Joshua 10:25). "Then you will prosper, if you are careful to follow the statutes and the ordinances which the Lord commanded Moses concerning Israel. Be strong and courageous, do not fear nor be dismayed." (I Chronicles 22:13). "Then David said to his son Solomon, "Be strong and courageous, and act; do not fear nor be dismayed, for the Lord God, my God, is with you. He will not fail you nor forsake you until all the work for the service of the house of the Lord is finished." (1 Chronicles 28:20). "Be strong and courageous, do not fear or be dismayed because of the king of Assyria nor because of all the horde that is with him; for the One with us is greater than the one with him." (2 Chronicles 32:7).

> "Wait for the Lord;
> Be strong and let your heart take courage;
> Yes, wait for the Lord." (Psalm 27:14).

> "Be strong and let your heart take courage,
> All you who wait for the Lord." (Psalm 31; 24,).

Majority of the Bible passages above emphasize the need for total commitment to God with strength and courage. In all the passages there is no room given to weakness and discouragement. This is a great instruction for humans in whatever endeavor they embark on to be strong and not to be discouraged. God knew that when unpleasant issues persist that humans have tendencies to lose heart, lose enthusiasm to push forward, they are prone to the propensity to back off from the battle with discouragement. Since God knew and still knows humans more than humans knew or know themselves, He gave and still gives humans the admonition to carry on with strength and courage. Humans are to be persistent in prayers seeking God's involvement in their battles. When humans are disheartened, momentarily, they are to be aware that life has its difficult times. Difficulties must be borne through the journey of life. However, humans should be rest assured that God would never abandon them in their struggles. Humans are to be confident that nothing is impossible with God. (Luke 1:37). However, humans are to exercise patience knowing that the Lord is always on their side and that He would win their battles for them if they abide, patiently, in faith, with Him. With God, humans are in the best hands. It is important to know, believe, and trust that God has 'their backs', therefore, to 'stay put.' When humans face battles they should be able to declare boldly, as Job did. "But He knows the way I take; When He has put me to the test, I will come out as gold." (Job 23:10). God understood his plight and overcame for him. In like manner Jesus understands human plight and He will overcome for them.

"In Jesus Name (God Of Possibility)

I speak the name of Jesus over you
In your hurting, in your sorrow
I will ask my God to move
I speak the name 'cause it's all that I can do
In desperation, I'll seek Heaven
And pray this for you

I pray for your healing
That circumstances would change
I pray that the fear inside would flee in Jesus name
I pray that a breakthrough would happen today
I pray miracles over your life in Jesus name, in Jesus name

I speak the name of all authority
Declaring blessings, every promise
He is faithful to keep
I speak the name no grave could ever hold
He is greater, He is stronger
He's the God of possible

I pray for your healing
That circumstances would change
I pray that the fear inside would flee in Jesus name
I pray that a breakthrough would happen today
I pray miracles over your life in Jesus name In Jesus name

Come believe it
Come receive it
Oh, the power of His Spirit is now forever yours
Come believe it
Come receive it
In the mighty name of Jesus, all things are possible

I pray for your healing
That circumstances will change
I pray that the fear inside will flee in Jesus name
I pray that a breakthrough
Would happen today
I pray miracles over your life in Jesus name
I pray for revival
For restoration of faith
I pray that the dead will come alive in Jesus name In Jesus name."
(Jeff Pardo, Ethan Hulse, David Andrew Spencer, Katy Nichole).

The Bible says, "for EVERYONE WHO CALLS ON THE NAME OF THE LORD WILL BE SAVED." (Romans 10:13). The name of Jesus is very powerful and could make evils disappear. It is important that humans call on the name of Jesus when battles rage around them and when they feel the peace and calmness from the presence of God.

Stay with the Lord, He understands your plight and He will overcome for you. However, God expects humans to do His will and follow His guidelines. Isaiah was clear in these proclamations, making it plain that humans are their own enemies in getting their battles resolved. At times, humans fail to follow the directives laid down by God, therefore, their sins might be in the way of their prayers.

> "Behold, the Lord's hand is not so short
> That it cannot save; Nor is His ear so dull
> That it cannot hear.
> But your wrongdoings have caused a separation between you and your God, And your sins have hidden His face from you so that He does not hear." (Isaiah 59:1–3).

Through David, God revealed what He requires of humans in order to be with Him and to get favor from Him. God expects humans to follow those directives from Him and all will be well with them. Their battles would not overcome them, but they would overcome their battles.

> "Who may ascend onto the hill of the Lord?
> And who may stand in His holy place?
> One who has clean hands and a pure heart,
> Who has not lifted up his soul to deceit
> And has not sworn deceitfully.
> He will receive a blessing from the Lord
> And righteousness from the God of his salvation.
> This is the generation of those who seek Him,
> Who seek Your face—even Jacob. Selah."
> (Psalm 24:24:3–6).

Is Greed In The Way Of Winning Your Battle?

"You ask and do not receive, because you ask with the wrong motives, so that you may spend what you request on your pleasures "(James 4:3). At times when humans pray to God and their prayers appears not to be answered, could it be that their requests were made for selfish reasons? God sees the heart of humans and He knows their motives. When humans are asking God to do anything for them based on selfish reasons, they might not get them because God knows best. Humans might not get what they are asking because God loves them and He knows that what they are asking of Him might lead to their destruction. Greediness only cares for self without giving consideration to the needs of others. Jesus was aware of the greediness of those who had possession and were hoarding them instead of sharing and helping those who are less fortunate like them. After watching the attitudes of the rich He warned them of their reliance on their possessions. "But He said to them, beware, and be on your guard against every form of greed; for not even when one is affluent does his life consist of his possessions. And He told them a parable, saying; The land of a rich man was very productive. And he began thinking to himself, saying, 'What shall I do, since I have no place to store my crops?' And he said, 'This *is* what I will do: I will tear down my barns and build larger ones, and I will store all my grain and my goods there.

And I will say to myself, "You have many goods stored up for many years to come; relax, eat, drink, and enjoy yourself! But God said to him, 'You fool! This very night your soul is demanded of you; and as for all that you have prepared, who will own it now?' Such is the one who stores up treasure for himself and is not rich in relation to God." (Luke 12:15–21).

Jesus was warning His hearers and all human beings not to rely on their possessions because those possessions are temporary and they possess no redeeming power. However, Jesus emphasized that what humans do for others with their possessions and to propagate the kingdom of God are the only things that will count in the kingdom of God. He then shared the experiences of the 'rich fool' who did not have plan for other human beings or for God on how to spend his blessings. Since he did not plan for anyone else and even not for God, but only for himself, his life was cut short. He did not have the benefit of all he had acquired. Words like I, I, I; Me, Me, Me; Mine, Mine, Mine are the telltale signs of selfishness, greediness, and the lack of caring for other human beings. In the teaching about the rich farmer his attention was only on himself and his planning was focused only on himself, but not on anyone else or on God. Humans should watch out not to be consumed by thinking only about themselves, but to always put others into consideration so they could get the blessings from God. "Do not store up for yourselves treasures on earth, where moth and rust destroy, and where thieves break in and steal. But store up for yourselves treasures in heaven, where neither moth nor rust destroys, and where thieves do not break in or steal; for where your treasure is, there your heart will be also." (Matthew 6:19–21). Jesus warned humans to be sure to store their treasure where they are safe, and where nothing could destroy them. The statement of where a person should put his or her treasure could be compared to people who invest their money in the stock market. Their mind is always on how the market trading is doing constantly. Their minds are always on their investment. However, in the case of investing in the stock market, an individual could gain or lose money. It is unstable and it goes up and down. However, any investment in heaven, in other human beings, and in the work of God are investments in heaven where it is stable. The ways to store one's treasure where it is safe are to invest those treasures in the lives of those who are needy and to invest them in promoting the kingdom of God. In order to satisfy that condition humans have to remove greediness in their lives. Jesus spoke in another teaching about the use of ones' possessions to help others and how one would be rewarded on the judgement day.

"Then the King will say to those on His right, 'Come, you who are blessed of My Father, inherit the kingdom prepared for you from the foundation of the world. For I was hungry, and you gave Me something to eat; I was thirsty, and you gave Me something to drink; I was a stranger, and you invited Me in; naked, and you clothed Me; I was sick, and you visited Me; I was in prison, and you came to Me. Then the righteous will answer Him, Lord, when did we see You hungry, and feed You, or thirsty, and give You *something* to drink? And when did we see You as a stranger, and invite You in, or naked, and clothe You? And when did we see You sick, or in prison, and come to You?' And the King will answer and say to them, 'Truly I say to you, to the extent that you did it for one of the least of these brothers or sisters of Mine, you did it for Me. Then He will also say to those on His left, 'Depart from Me, you accursed people, into the eternal fire which has been prepared for the devil and his angels; for I was hungry, and you gave Me nothing to eat; I was thirsty, and you gave Me nothing to drink; I was a stranger, and you did not invite Me in; naked, and you did not clothe Me; sick, and in prison, and you did not visit Me.' Then they themselves also will answer, Lord, when did we see You hungry, or thirsty, or as a stranger, or naked, or sick, or in prison, and did not take care of You?' Then He will answer them, 'Truly I say to you, to the extent that you did not do it for one of the least of these, you did not do *it* for Me, either.' These will go away into eternal punishment, but the righteous into eternal life." (Matthew 25:34–46). It is important for humans to know that their labor of generosity to others who could not pay them back is not forgotten by the Lord and He will reward them abundantly in this world and in the world to come. Therefore, the spirit of greediness should be removed far away from humans. Selfish spirit leads only to the thinking 'only of 'self.' When individuals' attention is turned inwardly and think only about themselves and have no room for others, it is only God Who could rescue them. Therefore, humans need to approach God to defeat the battle of greediness in their minds so they could share their love and possessions with others. When greediness has crept into humans' lives it is only the power of God that could remove it. Blessings come through generosity to others, but nothing good comes from hoarding. The Bible says, "One person gives freely, yet gains even more; another withholds unduly, but comes to poverty.

A generous person will prosper; whoever refreshes others will be refreshed." Proverbs 11:24–25, NIV). God appreciates and rewards those who give of their possessions to others and to promote His kingdom on earth. It is the gift which are not given grudgingly that God appreciates because it is freely given. It is neither given for selfish reasons nor by cohesion. The gift God appreciates to others or to promote His kingdom are those which are freely given. God is pleased with a cheerful giver., therefore, humans should remove greediness from themselves and freely give to others. Greediness leads to cheating, stealing and other evils, but by allowing the spirit of God to take control all those evil qualities will disappear. It is human to be greedy, but it is their submission to God that removes greediness from their minds. Therefore, humans need to submit their will to God to defeat greediness in their lives.

Fighting Your battle with Humility

Humility, is one of the personality traits God expects and admonishes humans to have. "The reward of humility and the fear of the Lord are riches, honor, and life." (Proverbs 22:4). "Humble yourselves in the presence of the Lord, and He will exalt you." (James 4:10). The two passages above confirm what God thinks of the trait of humility in human beings. When humans have humility, they give reference to God in whatever they do and God rewards them with riches, honor, and life. In addition to God's reward as stated above is His assistance to them in fighting their battles when they approach Him for help with reference and humility. God honors human humility in fighting battles. "You younger men, likewise, be subject to your elders; and all of you, clothe yourselves with humility toward one another, because GOD IS OPPOSED TO THE PROUD, BUT HE GIVES GRACE TO THE HUMBLE." (1 Peter 5:5). In order to be exalted and for God to be on their side in fighting their battles, humans need to conduct themselves with the spirit of humility. God's plan for humans is for them to live together in harmony regardless of age, ethnicity, or the sexual grouping of the individuals. "Be of the same mind toward one another; do not be haughty in mind but associate with the lowly. Do not be wise in your own estimation." (Romans 12:16). If humans abide by the guidelines regarding humility set by God, there could be less relational battles for humans to fight. In that case humans' relational issues and headaches might be reduced. "The reward of humility and the fear of the Lord are riches, honor, and life." (Proverbs 22:4). Humans are to pray to God to give them the spirit of humility. The benefits accompanying humility are honor and life.

"Therefore, humble yourselves under the mighty hand of God, so that He may exalt you at the proper time, having cast all your anxiety on Him, because He cares about you." (1 Peter 5:6–7). Humans need to show the spirit of humbleness when approaching God to assist them in whatever battle they are fighting. The Bible encourages the spirit of humbleness with a promise that, although, victory might not come as quickly as humans expect, but it will come, eventually, if humans are persistent. It might not come at humans' timetable, but at God's time. Humans are not to trust their own understanding, but they are to cast all their anxieties on Him. The Bible expects humans not to hold back some of their anxieties while giving some to the Lord, but to surrender all to God. They are to humble themselves well enough before God that they are not holding anything back from Him. They are to give all so that God could fight all their battles for them. The Bible also confirms that God cares for His creatures as a proof for them not to hold anything back from Him, but to give Him all their worries and battles. God has always been clear and not ambiguous about His wish for humans to be humble. God makes it a requirement for humans to be in good standing with Him and with other human beings. Listening to a moderator on a radio station, he mentioned his recollection of a remark he heard from someone saying, "he was not marveling at the bigness of God, but at the smallness of God." A first glance at this statement might give a mixed and confusing meaning without looking at the intended implication of the statement. Breaking down the two parts of the statement, one could see the implication of the statement. The first part of the statement deals with the bigness of God. Referencing the big things God does is marveling with fact that He has the whole world in His hands. God has bigger responsibilities for the whole world at a time. This is the bigger picture.

He's Got the Whole World in His Hands
He's got the whole world in his hands.
He's got the whole wide world in his hands.
He's got the whole world in his hands.
He's got the whole world in his hands.
He's got the wind and the rain in his hands.
He's got the wind and the rain in his hands.
He's got the wind and the rain in his hands.
He's got the whole world in his hands.
He's got the little bitty baby in his hands.
He's got the little bitty baby in his hands.
He's got the little bitty baby in his hands.
He's got the whole world in his hands.
He's got you and me sister in his hands.
He's got you and me sister in his hands.
He's got you and me sister in his hands.
He's got the whole world in his hands.
He's got ev'rybody in his hands.
He's got ev'rybody in his hands.
He's got ev'rybody in his hands.
He's got the whole world in his hands.
(African American Spiritual: <u>Young Women Camp Songs</u>).

However, the other part of the statement is the smaller parts of God's responsibilities, this is called the smallness of God. This statement about the smallness of God does not imply that God is small in any way, but it is referring to the minute details pertaining to His creation to which He pays attention. God does not forget any of His creation and that character of God should marvel humans. It should give humans encouragement to feel comfortable presenting their battles to Him regardless of how big or how small they are. They should have the assurance that God cares for them and will attend to their battles regardless of how few or how many they are. Jesus pointed out this fact vividly the fact that God cares for all his creation in these statements: "Look at the birds of the sky, that they do not sow, nor reap, nor gather crops into barns, and yet your heavenly Father feeds them. Are you not much more important than they? And which of you by worrying can add a single day to his life's span?" (Matthew 6:26–27). When humans face certain battles, they could feel helpless and allow anxiety to take over their thoughts rather than giving them to God. In that case they become paralyzed in doing anything to improve their lot by going to God. Jesus was reminding His hearers that God cares for them and instead of worrying, they should take their concerns about their battles to God who cares for them. Humans should not think that they are burdening God with their small battles when God has bigger battles to fight for other people. Such thinking is limiting the power of God who is able to fight all battles, big or small at the same time and at all times. Humans might be cutting short their blessings by holding on to their battle with the consideration that they do not want to burden God. God wants to hear about the needs of all, whether big or small because He could handle all of them according to His will. God wants to hear from all and His ears are attentive to the petitions of all humans. "They looked unto Him and were radiant; and their faces shall never be confounded.... The eyes of the Lord are toward the righteous, and His ears are toward their cry for help." (Psalm 34:15). "For the eyes of the Lord are toward the righteous and His ears attend to their prayer (1 Peter 3:12a). The passages above are evidence that God is eagerly waiting and eager for humans to approach Him with sincerity of hearts for their battles because His ears are open to receive their petitions. Therefore, when humans perceive that their battles are too small to take to God, they are denying God of His willingness to win their battles for them. Humans should not short-change themselves by not approaching God with their battles. Although those battles might be perceived by humans to be small, they need to realize that God is delighted in resolving small battles. They also need to know that God is a Specialist in resolving big battles. Therefore, whether your battles are small or big, take them all to the Lord Who is willing to resolve and win them for you. Moses was humble in his response to the rebellion which surfaced in his family. "Then Miriam and Aaron spoke against Moses because of the Cushite woman whom he had married (for he had married a Cushite woman); and they said, is it a fact that the Lord has spoken only through Moses? Has He not spoken through us as well? And the LORD heard this. (Now the man Moses was very humble, more than any person who was on the face of the earth.) And the LORD suddenly said to Moses and to Aaron and Miriam, you three go out to the tent of meeting. So, the three of them went out. Then the LORD came down in a pillar of cloud and stood at the entrance of the tent; and He called Aaron and Miriam. When they had both come forward, He said,

> Now hear My words:
> If there is a prophet among you,
> I, the LORD, will make Myself known to him in a vision.
> I will speak with him in a dream.
> It *is* not this way *for* My servant Moses;
> He is faithful in all My household;
> With him I speak mouth to mouth,
> That is, openly, and not using mysterious language,
> And he beholds the form of the LORD.
> So why were you not afraid
> To speak against My servant, against Moses?

And the anger of the LORD burned against them and He departed. But when the cloud had withdrawn from above the tent, behold, Miriam was leprous, as white as snow. As Aaron turned toward Miriam, behold, she was leprous. Then Aaron said to Moses, Oh, my lord, I beg you, do not hold us responsible for this sin by which we have turned out to be foolish, and by which we have sinned. Oh, do not let her be like a dead person, whose flesh is half eaten away when he comes out of his mother's womb! So, Moses cried out to the LORD, saying, God, heal her, please! But the LORD said to Moses, if her father had only spit in her face, would she not be put to shame for seven days? Have her shut outside the camp for seven days, and afterward she may be received again. So, Miriam was shut outside the camp for seven days, and the people did not move on until Miriam was received again. (Numbers 12:1–15). Aaron and Miriam, his brother and sister reviled and slandered him before the Israelites and before the Lord. There could have been some jealousy going on between his brother and sister against him (Moses). They attacked Moses and wanted him demoted.

They were hoping to replace him as the leader of the Israelites. This was an overthrow orchestrated by those who were close to Moses. It was an insurrection in the family of Moses. Moses could have asked God to punish them for their disloyalty to him, but he left his battle to the Lord to fight for him. He demonstrated the spirit of humility to those who were acting against him. Moses did not allow his pride to be in the way of giving his battle to the Lord to fight. Moses remained meek in the face of his betrayal by the members of his family and he handed his issues to the Lord and he trusted the Lord to handle them. When the punishment of the rebellion of his family was coming down on them Moses asked God for leniency and mercy on the perpetrators. (Numbers 12:1–15). Moses was exemplary in his meekness and humility as attested to by the scripture. There was a lesson with God's action and methodology in handling the issues which arose between Moses' brother and sister. This example should be emulated by anyone in the position of leadership. When God was aware of what Moses' brother and sister did, He called them into a meeting privately with only the three of them and no one else present. God passed His judgements on the perpetrators privately. The lesson for those in leadership or in authority is that it is important to resolve private issues privately between those involved only to restore relationship instead of dealing with the issue publicly and bringing shame and resentment to those involved. Jesus said, "Now if your brother sins, go and show him his fault in private; if he listens to you, you have gained your brother...." (Matthew 18:15). Hannah endured much humiliation because she was baren., "And her rival provoked her sore, to make her fret, because Jehovah had shut up her womb." (1 Samuel 1:6). She was harassed repeatedly for years by Peninnah, the other wife of her husband, who had children (1 Samuel 1:7). During their annual travel to the temple Shiloh, Hannah prayed to the Lord in her deep distress and bitterness, humbly sharing her heart with the Lord. Hannah went to the Lord with boldness of heart without any fear of asking God to give her a child. God answered her request and gave her a son, named Samuel. Hannah was so distressed with her battle of lack of a child that she prayed and wept with such zeal that

Eli, the priest, thought that she was drunk at the early part of the day. Hannah demonstrated her humility to the priest by clearly explaining her battle to him. She also made a humbly promise to the Lord that she would give the child she was requesting to the service of the Lord. "So, Hannah rose up after they had eaten in Shiloh, and after they had drunk. Now Eli the priest was sitting upon his seat by the doorpost of the temple of Jehovah. And she was in bitterness of soul, and prayed unto Jehovah, and wept sore. And she vowed a vow, and said, O Jehovah of hosts, if thou wilt indeed look on the affliction of thy handmaid, and remember me, and not forget thy handmaid, but wilt give unto thy handmaid a man-child, then I will give him unto Jehovah all the days of his life, and there shall no razor come upon his head. And it came to pass, as she continued praying before Jehovah, that Eli marked her mouth. Now Hannah, she spake in her heart; only her lips moved, but her voice was not heard, therefore, Eli thought she had been drunken. And Eli said unto her, how long wilt thou be drunken? put away thy wine from thee. And Hannah answered and said, no, my lord, I am a woman of a sorrowful spirit: I have drunk neither wine nor strong drink, but I poured out my soul before Jehovah. Count not thy handmaid for a wicked woman; for out of the abundance of my complaint and my provocation have I spoken hitherto. Then Eli answered and said, go in peace; and the God of Israel grant thy petition that thou hast asked of him. And she said, let thy handmaid find favor in thy sight. So, the woman went her way, and did eat; and her countenance was no more sad." (1 Samuel 1:9–18). David had some opportunities to kill Saul when Saul was vulnerable, however, David was humble enough to spare Saul's life in those occasions. Instead of harming Saul, David spared Saul's life but in order to remove all doubts about his opportunity to have killed Saul, so he cut a piece of Saul's robe (1 Samuel 24:4). Saul had been pursuing David for some time in order to kill him and David was aware of Saul's intent to kill him. However, David was humble and respectful of the Lord's anointed and because he believed Saul to be God's anointed he held himself back from killing Saul when opportunities availed themselves. (1 Samuel 24:5–6). There were similar opportunities for David to have avenged on his enemy who had been pursuing him with the intent to kill him, but he refrained from getting revenge and he humbled himself before the Lord. Even with Sauls's hatred for David, he still called Saul his Lord and king and he bowed down his face to Saul. He had the opportunities to kill Saul and take over the throne as the king in the place of Saul, however, he refrained and humbled himself and he "bowed his face and paid homage to Saul." (1 Samuel 24:8). In order that Saul could not doubt how close he was from being killed by David if not for David's humbleness, greed-lessness, and compassion for him, he would have been a dead man, David showed him the elm of his robe which he caught while Saul was asleep. David even addressed him as his father. (1 Samuel 24:11–12). David declared that he did not have any malice towards Saul and he made plain to Saul that he had not done any wrong to him and that the Lord would judge between both of them. David was in line with the admonition of Jesus: "You have heard that it was said, 'YOU SHALL LOVE YOUR NEIGHBOR and hate your enemy.' But I say to you, love your enemies and pray for those who persecute you, so that you may prove yourselves to be sons of your Father who is in heaven; for He causes His sun to rise on the evil and the good, and sends rain on the righteous and the unrighteous. For if you love those who love you, what reward do you have? Even the tax collectors, do they not do the same? And if you greet only your brothers and sisters, what more are you doing than others? Even the Gentiles, do they not do the same? Therefore, you shall be perfect, as your heavenly Father is perfect." (Matthew 5:43–48). God fought David's battle because he was humble and because of his invitation for God to fight his battle. David eventually did become king of Israel in God's perfect timing, not his own. This is a great example for humans to humble themselves, avoid revenge, and trust God who could win their battles for them successfully.

Abigail was a beautiful and discerning lady (1 Samuel 25:3). His husband, Nabal, was rich but he was harsh and bad mannered. "David had done a big kindness in looking after Nabal's shepherds and Carmel and he sent word to Nabal asking for food and drink for his men in return. Nabal, however, thought David's request was absurd, and he demeaned David. This angered David so much that he set out to kill all the males that belonged to Nabal. Thankfully, one of the shepherds informed Abigail about all that was taking place, and Abigail immediately went into action—she gathered up generous portions of food and wine for David and his men and traveled with her servants to meet David: When Abigail saw David, she hurried and got down from the donkey and fell before David on her face and bowed to the ground." (1 Samuel 25:23). David was not only overwhelmed by the humility and respect Abigail showed toward him, but he was also thankful to Abigail for keeping him from blood guiltiness. He obeyed Abigail's voice, granted her petition, and later married Abigail after the Lord struck Nabal dead soon afterward. Here are some of the words Abigail spoke to David in her petition: And now let this present that your servant has brought to my lord be given to the young men who follow my lord. Please forgive the trespass of your servant. For the Lord will certainly make my lord a sure house because my lord is fighting the battles of the Lord, and evil shall not be found in you so long as you live. If men rise up to pursue you and to seek your life, the life of my lord shall be bound in the bundle of the living in the care of the Lord your God. And the lives of your enemies he shall sling out as from the hollow of a sling." (1 Samuel 25:27–29). Abigail is one of the shining examples in the Scripture of what it means to be a godly woman who fears the Lord. Showing the spirit of humility could easily avert wars and broken relationships with humans and with God. Humility before God could make it easier for humans to get their battles taken over by God and make it His own battle thus relieving humans the burdens and hardships associated with battles.

Isaiah had a vision that he saw the Lord sitting upon His throne in the temple. "Isaiah immediately recognizes his total unworthiness to be in the presence of God and he says the following words: And I said: Woe is me! For I am lost; for I am a man of unclean lips, and I dwell in the midst of a people of unclean lips; for my eyes have seen the King, the Lord of hosts! One of God's seraphim flies over to Isaiah with a burning coal he has taken from the altar with tongs. The seraphim place the coal on Isaiah's lips so that Isaiah's guilt will be taken away and his sin atoned for

(Isaiah 6:5–7). Isaiah was very humble in declaring that he was a sinner. In fact, Isaiah declared that it was not only that he was a sinner, but his companions were all sinners. Isaiah saw himself as being doomed because of sins and because of the influence of those with whom he lived. When humans are in the presence of the living God, they realize their filthiness, their nakedness, and their unfitness to be before the Lord. This feeling occurred to Isaiah who considered himself unfit to present himself before the Lord. However, because of his humbleness the Lord came to his rescue. God cleansed him in order for him to be presentable to Him. The Lord won the battle of the separation between him and God and he became worthy to be in the presence of the Lord. The account of Daniel in the lion's den demonstrated how God did/does not forget His own but always came/comes to their rescue at the time when the battles for them are raging and when all hope is gone. All God wants humans to do is to be humble and trust Him. With the trust in God and humbleness to Him, He is always ever present to fight human battles. This was the case with Daniel when they were thrown into the den of lions because of their trust in God. Daniel decided to obey God and had his alliance with God above humans. He put God first and put obeying Him first and foremost. When the Israelite were in exile in Babylon, Daniel did not stop praying for their rescue. Daniel made it his battle to pray to God daily for the rescue of the Israelites from their bondage in Babylon. Despite the fact that King Darius signed a degree that no one in his jurisdiction should pray to any other God, but to the image he made. Daniel was not dissuaded from praying to the true God regardless of the consequences he could face, up to death. Daniel continued to pray to the true God in disregard to the king's decree. For his disobedience of the king's decree, he threw Daniel into the den of lions. Although Daniel's enemies tricked the king to sign the decree of severe punishment up to death for anyone who disobeyed him. The king had a regret carrying out the decree he signed against whoever disobeyed his decree. After throwing Daniel into the den of lion he felt so guilty that he might have caused the death of an innocent man and he was wishing that God would protect Daniel from the lions. Being thrown into the den of lions was the biggest battle of Daniels life, but he trusted God to fight his battle. God came through for Daniel and won his battle for him because he trusted God. God protected Daniel from all harm. The king knew with certainty that Daniel's God is the living God. The king declared to Daniel, "O Daniel, servant of the living God, has your God, whom you serve continually, been able to deliver you from the lions?" Then Daniel said to the king, O king, live forever! My God sent his angel and shut the lions' mouths, and they have not harmed me, because I was found blameless before him; and also, before you, O king, I have done no harm. Then the king was exceedingly glad, and commanded that Daniel be taken out of the den. So, Daniel was taken up out of the den, and no kind of harm was found on him, because he had trusted in his God." (Daniel 6:20–23). Paul, the apostle, held prestigious positions before becoming a Christian, as a Jew: "Though I myself have reason for confidence in the flesh also. If anyone else thinks he has reason for confidence in the flesh, I have more: circumcised on the eighth day of the people of Israel, of the tribe of Benjamin, a Hebrew of Hebrews; as to the law, a Pharisee; as to zeal, a persecutor of the church; as to righteousness under the law, blameless." (Philippians 3:4–6). Paul touted his heritage, his traditional accomplishments, and the good he has done, however, after meeting Jesus he realized that all those heritage, traditional achievements were not worthwhile in comparing to his believe in Christ. After meeting with the Lord all what he counted as gain became loss. All his achievements became like filthy rags in comparison to what the Lord provided him. "But whatever things were gain to me, these things I have counted as loss because of Christ. More than that, I count all things to be loss in view of the surpassing value of knowing Christ Jesus my Lord, for whom I have suffered the loss of all things, and count them *mere* rubbish, so that I may gain Christ, and may be found in Him, not having a righteousness of my own derived from the Law, but that which is through faith in Christ, the righteousness which *comes* from God on the basis of faith, that I may know Him and the power of His resurrection and the fellowship of His sufferings, being conformed to His death; if somehow I may attain to the resurrection from the dead." (Philippians 3:7–11).

The closer Paul moved to Jesus the less all the achievements in his life took any importance to him, but the love of Christ. Before Paul met Jesus, he used to consider himself very smart and important but after meeting Jesus all those things went to the second place in his life and he humbly followed Jesus. All the things which appeared as wisdom to him became foolishness. This is like the story of a family who were raising their children, however, at certain time when their children reached adolescent ages, they felt that they were wiser than them. Whenever their parents gave them the right way to do things or to behave in certain ways, they felt that they were wiser than their parents. The parents noticed that their children were no longer readily following their directions. At that stage of life their children felt that they knew better than their parents and that their parents' ideas were old. The parents endured the behaviors of their children and were hoping that the senses would one day come into their heads. Not long after their children started their college education, whenever issues arose in their college, they called their parents for directions on what to do. The parents were very satisfied with the humility which all of a sudden, their children were displaying, some sense got into the heads of their children. The parents praised God that all the training and examples they showed their children were bearing fruits. The children realized that all the wisdom that was important to them for which they were boasting about was nothing compared to the wisdom of their parents. If you are reading this book and you are frustrated about the know-all attitude of your teenage children, take solace in the fact that there will come a time that you will become wise parents in their sight, they will be seeking your pieces of advice which they may be reluctant to follow at this present time. Know that this time too will soon pass. There is an awareness that the more a person knows, the more the person realizes that he or she does not know much and that there is much more left for him or her to know. This is the case with Paul, the more he knew Jesus the more he humbled himself and the more he realized that which used to be important to him became minor, but the only thing that mattered to Paul was belonging to Christ. All who have faith in God should humbly approach Him and pray that the only thing that should matter to them is their faith in Him as their Savior.

Humans need to realize that there is nothing about them that is untouched by their infected sin nature and how unfit humans are to stand before God on their own worths—therefore humans should run to the foot of the cross and embrace Christ, their lasting hope. Humans could not depend on their own strength to overcome their battles, but the Lord could win those battles for them. "Trust in the Lord with all your heart And do not lean on your own understanding. In all your ways acknowledge Him, And He will make your paths straight." (Proverbs 3:5–6). Humans should not rely on their own ability, but on the strength which comes from the Lord. Peter relied on his own abilities and strengths and when those strengths and abilities failed him, he denied the Lord three times, not even once or twice but three times, and the cock crew. Sadly, when asked if he was a follower of Jesus on the night of Jesus' arrest, Peter denied even knowing his Lord not once but three times (Luke 22:54–62). His betrayal of Jesus caused Peter to weep bitterly and that is one of the most humbling accounts we find in the Bible. Yet, Jesus forgave Peter and the apostle went on to faithfully preach the gospel boldly at Pentecost (Acts 2:14–41) and did miracles in Jesus' name.

Angel Gabriel appeared to Mary to tell her that she would give birth to the "Son of the Most High," whose kingdom would have no end (Luke 1:26–33). Mary asked the angel how this could be since she was still a virgin: And the angel answered her, "The Holy Spirit will come upon you, and the power of the Most High will overshadow you; therefore the child to be born will be called holy—the Son of God. And behold, your relative Elizabeth in her old age has also conceived a son, and this is the sixth month with her who was called barren. For nothing will be impossible with God." And Mary said, "Behold, I am the servant of the Lord; let it be to me according to your word." And the angel departed from her. (Luke 1:35–38). Even though Mary was merely a young girl and greatly favored by God, her heart was focused on serving God and honoring

Him. In a beautiful song of praise known as the Magnificat, she gave thanks to the Lord for being chosen to bear the incarnate Son of God (Luke 1:46–55)."My soul magnifies the Lord

> My soul magnifies the Lord
> My spirit rejoices in God my Savior
> My soul magnifies the Lord
> My spirit rejoices in God
> Verse 2 (Basses join with:)
> Glory be to God the Father
> And glory be to God the Son
> Glory be to God the Spirit
> Glory be to God
> Verse 3 (altos join in with:)
> He has been mindful of His servant
> He has been mindful of me
> I will be blessed forever forever
> I will be blessed by the Lord
> Verse 4 (Tenors join in with...)
> God alone is mighty mighty
> Our God alone has done great things
> God alone is worthy worthy
> Holy is His name."
> (Gill, Randy, 200).

No one else could ever possess more humility or courage than Jesus. Even though He was God, He willingly humbled Himself to be born in the flesh to save humans from their guilt and condemnation. Jesus resolutely went to the cross and endured the most terrible torture and humiliation and shame ever, despite the fact that He was innocent: "Have this mind among yourselves, which is yours in Christ Jesus, who, though He was in the form of God, did not count equality with God a thing to be grasped, but emptied Himself, by taking the form of a servant, being born in the likeness of men. And being found in human form, he humbled Himself by becoming obedient to the point of death, even death on a cross. Therefore, God has highly exalted Him and bestowed on Him the name that is above every name, so that at the name of

Jesus every knee should bow, in heaven and on earth and under the earth, and every tongue confess that Jesus Christ is Lord, to the glory of God the Father." (Philippians. 2:5–11). Throughout the gospels, Jesus never sought power for Himself. He prayed to the Father to glorify Him so that He would bring glory to the Father (John 17:1–5). All that Jesus desired was everything that could glory God. Jesus showed humility every time when He could have taken glory for Himself. Due to His humility and submission to God He was able to overcome great battles for Himself and for those who submit themselves to Him. As Jesus overcame the battles for those believers then He is ready to win human battles at the present time only if humans submit themselves to Him and seek His assistance with their battles because the battle belongs to the Lord.

Fighting the Battle of Hatred

Hatred is a heavy load which weighs humans down and prevents them from being successful in battles. There are two sides to hatred, one is the positive connotation and the other is the negative side of hatred. The positive side deals with hating what God hates such as sin, but the negative side is hating other human beings. Hating sins keeps humans in alignment with God. When humans hate sin, they are going to refrain from committing it. When humans walk closely with the Lord and have fellowship with Him, the more aware they will be of sin, both inwardly and outwardly. When God's name is maligned, when humans see spiritual hypocrisy, plain unbelief, and godless behavior, humans should be appalled and angry at the action and not on the actors. The more humans understand God's attributes and love His character, the more they will be like Him and the more they will hate those things that are contrary to God's Word and nature. Hatred of other human being is not pleasing to God. This idea is confirmed by the Psalmist: "Hate evil, you who love the Lord, Who watches over the souls of His godly ones; He saves them from the hand of the wicked." (Psalm 97:10). Those who believe in God should be outraged, grieved, be angry when God's name is spoken ill of, when there is expression of spiritual hypocrisy, or when they observe Godless attitudes. The closer humans move to God the more they hate the work of sin and the more they love others. However, negative hatred is hatred directed against other human beings. Jesus warned His hearers to be careful of hating other people because of the consequences that could follow such hatred. Two things cannot occupy the same space at the same time, one could not profess to love God who one does not see and hate other human beings who one can see. Anyone who believes such is a liar and the service of the person is in vain and he or she is deceitful to himself or herself. "If someone says, I love God" and yet he hates his brother or sister, he is a liar; for the one who does not love his brother and sister whom he has seen, cannot love God, whom he has not seen. And this commandment we have from Him, that the one who loves God must also love his brother and sister." (1 John 4:2–21). Jesus warned humans of the consequences for hating other human beings when He said, "But, I say to you that everyone who is angry with his brother shall be answerable to the court; and whoever says to his brother, You good-for-nothing,' shall be answerable to the supreme court; and whoever says, 'You fool,' shall be guilty enough to *go* into the fiery hell.

"But I tell you that anyone who is angry with his brother will be subject to judgment" (Matthew 5:22). God does not condone hatred as could be seen in the statement in the following passage of the Bible. "The one who says that he is in the Light and yet hates his brother or sister is in the darkness until now…But the one who hates his brother or sister is in the darkness and walks in the darkness and does not know where he is going because the darkness has blinded his eyes. (1 John 2:9, 11). The Bible compared people who are full of hatred as being blind people because their hatred of others has blocked their vision. The situation is even worse for such people if they continue to profess religion while continuing in hatred of others. Although such people might lie and deceive others, but they could not deceive God. Eventually, such people would be found wanting after the vale is removed and the truth is known of their enmity and hatred being harbored against their fellow human beings. Hatred is a poison which destroys humans from within, resulting in bitterness which destroys human hearts and minds. Hatred removes humans from being in true relationship with God and with other human beings. "If we confess our sins, He is faithful and righteous, so that He will forgive us our sins and cleanse us from all unrighteousness. If we say that we have not sinned, we make Him a liar and His word is not in us. (1 John 1:9 –10). Let us be careful to do as the Lord advised and keep short accounts with everyone about everything, no matter how small, and the Lord will be faithful to forgive, as He has promised (1 John 2:1). Hatred is the disease of the heart which only God can cure. It is an hinderance preventing humans from being victorious over their battles. However, when humans confess their sins and move to God in repentance, the Lord will lead them to win their battle of hatred for nothing is impossible with God.

"Haters will see you walk on water and say it's because you can't swim. Whatever you do good or bad, your haters have something negative to say, always.

There is always someone behind you to appreciate and many to criticize, that's the human tendency. They hardly accept anyone's fame. They don't miss a single chance to dominate the potential of a high performer, they criticize him or her, they complained about him or her, throw the blaming 'bla bla bla.' Now you have to decide whether to sit quietly or to work harder than before. You have to decide whether to hear your inner voice or let the outside noise knock you down, whether to give up or to shut your haters up by your success. Of course, it needs a lot of courage, self-motivation, and a hunger to do something beyond the haters' imagination. It's not that easy to rise above all the odds but at the same time it's not impossible too. All you need is sheer dedication and focus. When people dislike or hate you for no apparent reason, it is most likely because you possess something that they don't or because your presence threatens their Ego. Whatever the case, let their hate motivate you to achieve an even higher ground of excellence. Use their anger towards you as the fuel to add the fire burning inside you. Let the flame rise up beyond anyone's capacity to control the heat. Have the courage to fight against all the Odds. Don't allow it to disturb your inner peace. (Priyanka Behuria). "If the world hates you, you know that it has hated Me before it hated you." (John 15:18). Jesus in His warning to His followers made the above statement in preparing them for what to expect. Jesus did not want it to be a surprise to His followers how people would accept and treat them. When humans are following the will of God they might be hated because of their devotion to God. That hatred might not be from people who are distant to them, but unfortunately it might be coming from the people close to them. It could be very disappointing and discouraging to experience such hatred. Jesus had felt such hatred from the people closer to Him, therefore, He was preparing his followers for the experiences which might come their ways. James followed with the words of encouragement for when humans are being hated when he said: "Consider it all joy, my brothers and sisters, when you encounter various trials, knowing that the testing of your faith produces endurance. And let endurance have its perfect result, so that you may be perfect and complete, lacking in nothing." James 1:2–4,). Being hated by others is a trial as much as it is a battle. It takes endurance to be able to skate through them unscathed. There is no human being who could possess such enduring power, but the Lord does. Endurance is vital in winning the battle of hatred from others. It is mind-boggling to consider trials as joy, how could trials be considered joy! When hatred is lumped together with other trials, why did James say to consider it all joy? What joy could be found in trials, in hatred received, and in battles experienced? The next question then is, why did James' admonish humans to consider it joy when they are facing various trials? The answers to the questions could be found by examining further James's admonition. First, he said that those trials are tests of the believers' faith. Those tests would produce endurance. It is like going to the gymnasium and lifting weights. At the beginning it is a test of how much one could lift. It appears to be very difficult at the initial stages of lifting, but as one endures, one could lift heavier weights for longer duration than at the beginning. In a similar manner, according to James, enduring trials increases the faith of the individual and produces joy. As one endures the rigor of lifting weight, the same endurance in weightlifting could propel the individual to other exercise activities requiring endurance. As time progresses an individual's endurance increases leading to joy in what the individual has achieved. The same is true of the endurance associated with the testing of one's faith. When humans endure the testing of their faith, they could look back and see the positive fruits of their labor of endurance and rejoice in the perfection which have come into their life. James in essence was admonish humans to endure tests of their faith because it improves their faith in God through the perfection which could come to them. The test of a person's faith could come inform of hatred (battle) for the individual, but by taking those tests and battles to God, an individual could become a victorious and rejoice in hope. It is less important how humans respond when things are going well compared to when things are not going well. In other words, how humans respond to other human beings when they are nice to them is less important than how they respond when other human beings are not nice to them. It has been said that if one wants to know what is inside an orange, one needs to put pressure on it. With pressure on an orange what is truly inside it will come out. When you are squeezed by the pressure of life, is what will come out of you going to be sweet or bitter? When you experience hatred from others will your endurance produce perfection in your faith, move you closer to God and to other people or will it drive you away from God and from other human beings? Consider your response and invite God to fight your battles for you so you could portray Christ in the midst of any hatred directed against you by other human beings.

People might hate another person or group because they are envious of them for what other people represent to them, because of what they have or because of their standing in society. They might feel that it is not fair that the other people or group have what they feel should be theirs. Therefore, they are contentious of those people or group. "When we see someone who even looks different from us, "there is preferential activation of the amygdala," which means the brain region associated with fear and aggression flares up. This visceral, emotional reaction can spark a long-term pattern of dislike when it's validated by action: if you perceive that someone has hurt you, your fear of them becomes rational. Our negative feelings toward someone get stronger as bad experiences with them pile up, and these negative thoughts trigger the fight-or-flight response in our bodies. (Robert Sapolsky). "Our fight-or-flight response is our bodies way of dealing with a stressor." (AJ Marsden). According to Marsden the fight-or-flight response might not be because of life-or-death situations but it could become a protective device against someone being hated for substantial or non-substantial reasons. Having to work or associate with someone who one hated could create such stress or and the need for self-protection. When this type of response continues for a while, it puts on human bodies and conditioning them to be more skeptical of other people's actions than they would be if they felt neutral about them says (Marsden). Even if they were to do something positive, the attention remains on the actual or the perceived negative perception because that is what the brain has been trained to perceive. This explains the reason humans have an endless list of negative facts about people whom they hate. They have trained their brain not to see any redeeming qualities in those they hate. The heightened awakening of human fearful disposition causes humans to be fearful of those they hate. Such feelings entrench humans deeper in their dislike of other people, thus validating their negative feelings. Marsden compared the hatred of others by saying, "in this way, our distaste for another person becomes like a snake eating its tail: we dislike them because they make us feel bad, and we feel bad because we dislike them. " But, since there's no "Black Mirror"-style real life-muting feature, we have to learn how to overcome dislike in order to get on with our daily lives. As Marsden points out, "our dislike tends to negatively impact our own behavior with co-workers and mutual friends: "If we don't like a person, we may be short with them or interrupt them without realizing it. They notice our rudeness toward them and often respond with rudeness, confirming our negative thoughts about that person." The key to breaking this vicious cycle, Marsden says, is mindfulness; when you're aware of how your dislike influences your body (and your behavior), you can start to condition yourself to respond rationally. When it comes to dislike, maybe "out of sight, out of mind, out of control" is a better-amended motto. Since dislike is rooted in a fear of the unknown, perhaps understanding more about where our dislike comes from can help us overcome its influence on our behavior. And when all else fails, there's always the 'block' feature." (Masrden)

Considering the statements and findings by Sapolsky and Marsden above, it appears that hatred and disliking other people is a battle of the heart. It is a disease of the heart which only God could cure. God who knows the heart of humans declared thus,

> "The heart is more deceitful than all else
> And is desperately sick;
> Who can understand it?
> I, the LORD, search the heart,
> I test the mind,
> To give to each person according to his ways,
> According to the results of his deeds."
> (Jeremiah 17:9–10).

There is a misconception which people believe to be true and by which they aspire to live their lives thinking that it is the right way to guide their lives. When taking literally or biologically, the fallacy of this belief and statement is that the heart does not have a thinking ability. The heart is just a muscular pump moving blood throughout the body by the energy provided from another organ. Therefore, the heart has no decision to make in pumping the blood throughout the body which is its main function. If the heart is unable to decide about its own function, how could it direct or lead others to follow it in doing anything? It is as the Bible says regarding the blind leading the blind, they will all fall into a ditch. "Leave them alone; they are blind guides of blind people. And if a person who is blind guides another who is blind, both will fall into a pit." (Matthew 15:14). Therefore, the statement advising people to follow their hearts could be a misguided statement when looked at from one point of view. However, when looked at it from another point of view the heart could be equated to the mind. According to Linda Luke, "When we are racing through our days, we lose the guidance of our hearts and are more likely to make unconscious choices that do not serve us well. Because our hearts process things much slower than our minds. See what I mean. Your mind moves much faster than your heart. Have you felt it? Your heart trying to catch up with your mind or being completely lost along the way? Your mind is running the show, but it's running blindly without connecting to the most powerful source that keeps you grounded in who you are and what is right for you. Most of us have an intention to live and make decisions from our hearts. We want to consciously choose what we create in our lives and know that letting our heart guide us is the best way to make that happen. But, we have to slow down so that we can hear what our heart has to say. The way to be sure is to allow time in your daily life to reconnect with your inner knowing and let your heart guide you. All of the answers are there if you just listen." There is a misconception in the statement "Follow Your Hearts." The statement to follow your heart and to let your heart lead you is contrary to the statement in the Bible that … Humans cannot even understand the wickedness of their own hearts and since that is the truth, humans do not have the ability to win the wickedness of their own hearts. Since humans are powerless to win the wickedness of their own hearts, they are doomed to losing the battle. However, by submitting to God, He could lead humans to victory over the wickedness and the hatred resulting from their hearts. Hatred is a sin which acts like cancer which festers and destroys humans gradually or rapidly from within, leading to bitterness and destruction of the mind and body. "See to it that no one comes short of the grace of God; that no root of bitterness springing up causes trouble, and by it many become defiled;" (Hebrews 12:15). "If we confess our sins, He is faithful and righteous, so that He will forgive us our sins and cleanse us from all unrighteousness." (1 John 1:9). The warning in Hebrews is plainly clear that hatred could make humans lose the grace provided by God by living in hatred of others instead of loving them. Hatred could lead to bitterness and unhappiness between humans. Therefore, humans should confess the sin of hatred and receive the forgiveness which comes from God. When humans confess their sin of hatred and are forgiven of their sin of it, then they could move freely to God to help hem fight other battles in their lives and win.

Role of Love in Fighting Battle.

The love of Jesus Christ covers all human sins, there is no other who has the power to cover human sins. However, Christ expects humans to be like Him, especially, those humans who have accepted Him as their Lord and Savior. To be like Jesus, humans need to love their enemies and those who treat them badly. Humans are to show love not only to those who are nice or love them, but even to those who treat them with hatred. Peter admonished humans by saying; "Above all, keep fervent in your love for one another, because love covers a multitude of sins." (1 Peter 4:8). Similar sentiment is expressed in proverb; "Hatred stirs up strife, But love covers all offense" (Proverbs 10:12). How can humans fight the battle of lack of love for those who have treated them badly? In fighting the battle of lack of love they need to know that it is impossible for humans to express love to those who have treated them poorly and with contempt. However, everything is possible with God and He could create new hearts in humans to love their enemies. Some humans have faced challenges which appear to be impossible to overcome. There could be joyous relief when humans' belief and practice are grounded in scriptural insight. Even in some untenable ugly circumstances, the Lord could get those who are obedient to His counsel out of such circumstances unscathed. "Love is patient, love is kind, it is not jealous; love does not brag, it is not arrogant. It does not act disgracefully, it does not seek its own benefit; it is not provoked, does not keep an account of a wrong suffered," (1 Corinthians 13:4–5)

"I Don't Deserve It

I wanna look confident, I wanna be tough
I spent 24 years alone, hiding from everyone
But then you came along and we fell in love
I'm not used to being seen this much by anyone

I've been invisible since I was a child
I'm good at comforting myself when I cry
And all this time I didn't know the reason why
But I can see it now with you by my side

When you look at me
When you ask me how I'm doing
When you take the time to get to know me
It's all too much

When you talk to me
It's the simple things that kill me
And I love the way you love me
But I feel like I don't deserve it
I don't deserve it

The way I see myself, it isn't right
Undeserving, so unworthy of a minute of your time
And I just can't be myself, I try so hard
I want to earn love and affection so I play my part

I've been invisible since I was a child
It's hard to sit here now and let you see me cry
And yeah it's painful always keeping this inside
But when you look into my eyes I wanna run and hide

When you look at me
When you ask me how I'm doing
When you take the time to get to know me
It's all too much

When you talk to me
It's the simple thing that kill me
And I love the way you love me
But I feel like I don't deserve it

I feel like I deserve to be alone
I feel like I am worst than everyone
And I've always felt this way
But you still love me as I am
You still want me and I just don't understand

When you look at me
When you ask me how I'm doing
When you take the time to get to know me
It's all too much
When you talk to me
It's the simple things that kill me
And I love the way you love me
But I feel like I don't deserve it

When you look at me
When you ask me how I'm doing
When you take the time to get to know me
It's all too much
When you talk to me
It's the simple things that kill me
And I love the way you love me
But I feel like I don't deserve it

I love the way you love me
But I feel like I don't deserve it
I don't deserve it."
(Lisa Cimorelli).

Humans do not deserve the love which God bestowed and which He continues to bestow on them daily. God has so much love for His creation that he did not wait on humans to be right with Him before He rescued them from the impending condemnation. "For while we were still helpless, at the right time Christ died for the ungodly. For one will hardly die for a righteous person, though perhaps for the good person someone would even dare to die. But God demonstrates His own love toward us, in that while we were still sinners, Christ died for us. (Romans 5:6–8,).

God made humans righteous through His righteousness. Humans have nothing to contribute to the righteousness which they receive from God because it is the gift of God to them. By human standard an accused has to pay penance before being freed, however, with God the sinners' penance was paid by someone else, the son of God. God did not wait for humans to go to Him first, but He came down to humans and reached out to safe them. God projected His love to humans by saving them when they did not deserve to be saved, but because God did not want anyone to be destroyed therefore, He made provision to save all who go to Him in repentance. "See how great a love the Father has bestowed on us, that we would be called children of God; and such we are." (1 John 3:1). The love God had for humans was so great that He invited humans into His family as His children. God adopted humans into His holy family, but in order to fit where there was no sin, Christ cleaned up humans of their sins by washing them with His blood. "… having canceled out the certificate of debt consisting of legal demands [which were in force] against us and which were hostile to us. And this certificate He has set aside and completely removed by nailing it to the cross." (Colossians 2:14, AB). God's love is never ending, it continued from the beginning of creation, it will endure to the end of the earth, and it will continue into eternity. "Beloved, let's love one another; for love is from God, and everyone who loves has been born of God and knows God. The one who does not love does not know God, because God is love. By this the love of God was revealed in us, that God has sent His only Son into the world so that we may live through Him. In this is love, not that we loved God, but that He loved us and sent His Son to be the propitiation for our sins. Beloved, if God so loved us, we also ought to love one another." (1 John 4:7–11) John pointed out that because of God's great love for humans, there is no excuse for humans not to love their fellow human beings. God has set a great example of His indiscriminate love for all humans; therefore, humans should extend similar indiscriminatory love to others. John stated further in his discourse that knowing God is loving others and whenever a person does not display genuine love to others it is an indication that such a person does not know God. "Love is patient and kind; love does not envy or boast; it is not arrogant or rude. It does not insist on its own way; it is not irritable or resentful; it does not rejoice at wrongdoing but rejoices with the truth." (1 Corinthians 13:4–8a, (ESV). The above message from Paul could be interpreted to mean that in order to express genuine love to others, humans need to get God involved in removing the battle of the mind associated with boasting or pride, domineering attitude, irritability, and resentment. It is only by having clean minds that humans could express true love to others. Lack of love for other human beings is an indication of the battle raging inside an individual. It is only through an individual submission to God that the fire of lack of love in the individual could be exterminated. The Psalmist realized that by his own power he could do nothing worthwhile, therefore, he pleaded to the Lord to create a new heart in him. The Psalmist realized that the battle inside him was an unclean heart and he was begging God to give him victory over his battle of unclean heart by giving him a heart transplant. The Psalmist realized that the connective tissues and blood vessels to his heart had been corrupted and that nothing good could come out of it, therefore, he needed a new and clean heart because his old heart had been clogged up with sin. The Psalmist was afraid that he was becoming useless to God and that he was in the brink of being discarded by God, therefore, he earnestly prayed to God not to cast him away. The Psalmist realized that he had a wayward spirit and for that he prayed to God for a steadfast spirit. He realized that joy of his salvation had disappeared, therefore he was begging God to give it back to him.

> "Create in me a clean heart, God,
> And renew a steadfast spirit within me.
> Do not cast me away from Your presence,
> And do not take Your Holy Spirit from me.
> Restore to me the joy of Your salvation,

And sustain me with a willing spirit." Psalm 51:10–12). Reading the above statement and the pleading by the Psalmist, one would realize that he lost the relationship he had had with the Lord and he missed that relationship greatly. He lost his great relationship with God because of pride, the sin of selfishness, and the lack of genuine love for his fellow human beings. Although he was lost in the wilderness of sin, he found his way back to God and he pleaded to God to conquer for him the battle of his sins. The Lord restored him and He won his battle for him. If you are fighting the battle of lack of love by yourself, in your own power, know plainly that you are not able to win your battle unless you ask God to transplant in you the heart of love and the spirit of steadfastness. Christ died for sinners who were living below the standard set by God as a commitment between Him and God to be the sacrificial lamb to save them even when they do not deserve His saving grace. Jesus extended His saving grace unto humans due to His love for them, even when they did not deserve it. The love God had for his creature was so great that He overlooked their shortcomings to redeem them from destruction. God is the One who justifies; humans cannot justify themselves. Humans are too weak and helpless to fight their own battles. Humans are not strong or good enough to live a life to satisfy God's standards of the way to live, therefore, Christ died to prop up humans to the standard expected of humans by God. Christ death was necessary to bring up humans to the standard set by God. Christ did not die for those who were godly, for those who were living up to God's standard, but for those who have fallen short of the glory of God. Humans were living ungodly life and bringing them back to God requires the death of Christ which Christ underwent voluntarily. Christ's death for sinners was willingly and timely because it came at the right time. Therefore, when humans are praying to God for certain needs and they have not got the answer the way they desire and at the time they want, they need to believe and take solace in the fact that God does things at the right time. God showed His love to humans by saving them in their helpless state through the death of Christ. God expects humans to replicate similar love to their fellow human beings so as to overcome their battles.

Dr. David Ajeigbe

"…Yes, mighty One

Mighty One
We worship You
Yes, mighty One
Mighty One
We worship You

… For I've tasted and seen Your goodness
And I've stood in the power of Your presence
For I've felt the depths of Your mercy
And oh, how Your love, it always surrounds me

… Oh, mighty One (You are, You are)
Mighty One (yes)
We worship You (strong and mighty One)
Mighty One (yeah)
Mighty One
We worship You

… For I've tasted and seen Your goodness
And I've stood in the power of Your presence
For I've felt the depths of Your mercy
And oh, how Your love, it always surrounds me
(For I've) for I've tasted and seen Your goodness
And I've stood in the power of Your presence
(And I've felt) for I've felt the depths of Your mercy
And oh, how Your love, it always surrounds me

… You alone
Are worthy of
The highest praise
And all my love
For You alone
Are worthy of
The highest praise
And all my love
For You alone
Are worthy of
The highest praise

How Do You Fight Your Battle?!!!

And all my love
For You alone
Are worthy of (You alone are worthy of)
The highest praise (the highest praise)
And all my love
Oh, for You alone
Are worthy of (yeah)
The highest praise (yeah)
And all my love
(Sing, "You alone") for You alone
Are worthy of
The highest praise (yeah)
And all my love
(Come on, You alone) Oh, You alone
Are worthy of
Oh, the highest praise
And all my love
For You alone
Are worthy of
The highest praise (you alone are worthy)
And all my love (you alone are worthy, You alone)
For You alone
Are worthy of
The highest praise
And all my love (yeah)

… For I've tasted and seen Your goodness
And I've stood in the power of Your presence
For I've felt the depths of Your mercy
Oh, how Your love, it always surrounds me (it always surrounds me)
It always surrounds me

… Can You feel His love surround us?
Can You feel His love embrace us?
It's not like man-made love
It's not like human love
Something supernatural
Something supernatural
It's mighty love

It's mighty love
What mighty love, what mighty love
It surrounds, it surrounds, it surrounds, it surrounds us

… For I've tasted and seen Your goodness
And I've stood in the power of Your presence
For I've felt the depths of Your mercy
Oh, how Your love, it always surrounds me"
(Dante Bowe / Mitch Wong / Todd Dulaney).

The type of love which was in existence before humans realized God's love, was old and self-centered. The type of love which humans were used to was to love those who have shown love to them and to hate those who have hated them. It was a conditional love which people were practicing. However, Jesus' presence changed that mindset when He gave a new commandment with regards to love by the expression and practice of it. In Jesus' teaching He said, "I am giving you a new commandment, that you love one another; just as I have loved you, that you also love one another. By this all people will know that you are My disciples: if you have love for one another." (John 13:34–35). Jesus wanted His followers to show love to others so that love exists between each of them. Following Christ would be more attractive to those who have not been His follower when they observe the love being expressed among His followers. Their expression of love would validate the example Jesus had set as being genuine. With such impression others would be interested in following Christ because they would like to enjoy the benefit of the love being displayed. Jesus was teaching His followers to be examples of good deeds demonstrated by their love. Jesus wanted His followers to present Him well to others in high regard. It is just like parents who instruct their children to represent their family well whenever they are outside the home. Parents know that the behavior of their children has a good or bad reflection on them and on their family. Many groups identify themselves in different ways such as by their ethnic group, their skin color, their language, their geographical locations, their occupation, their country of origin, their sex, their marital status, their community status or any other status, however, Jesus, determined and demonstrated the only identity important to God and beneficial to humans is their deep, sincere love for brothers and sisters in Christ. " Be kind to one another, compassionate, forgiving each other, just as God in Christ also has forgiven you." (Ephesians 4:32). Paul continued the principle left by Jesus in the above statement by emphasizing kindness embedded in love for each other. But God demonstrates His own love toward us, in that while we were still sinners, Christ died for us. Much more then, having now been justified by His blood, we shall be saved from the wrath of God through Him. For if while we were enemies we were reconciled to God through the death of His Son, much more, having been reconciled, we shall be saved by His life." (Romans 5:8–10). Jesus demonstrated an unconditional love which He expects his followers to practice unconditionally and sacrificially to other human beings, especially, to those who are His followers. In a teaching, Jesus compared himself to the vine and His followers to the branches. In that teaching He encouraged His followers to abide in Him so they could bear fruit. (John 15:1–5). The types of fruit Jesus was referring to are love, joy, peace, patience, kindness, goodness, faithfulness, gentleness, self-control; against which is no condemnation. (Galatians 5:22–23).

It is unnatural for humans to love as Christ wants them to love. For humans to hate gives immediate, but temporary satisfaction for the wrong actually done or perceived. Lack of love is a sin, and it is a battle for humans to conquer, however, it is impossible to overcome this battle and win without the involvement of God. Therefore, in order to love others, humans need God to intervene and win the battle of hatred for them and replace it with the joy of love. When God intervene in human life characterized by new capacity to love like Christ loves unconditionally, forgiving any wrong sacrificially, and forever. Loving as Christ loves is a sign of being disciples and followers of Christ. To love one another is to love fellow believers as Christ loves them. Those who love like Christ in the Holy Spirit's power will give evidence that they are disciples, or learners, of Jesus Christ.

Role of unforgiveness in Fighting Battle.

"Treat people the same way you want them to treat you." (Luke 6:31).

"In everything, therefore, treat people the same way you want them to treat you, for this is the Law and the Prophets." Matthew 7:12).

In the two messages from Jesus, He wanted His hearers to consider how they would want other people to treat them. Jesus knew what is pleasurable to humans and what things they would expect others to do to them, therefore, He wants humans to do similar things to other people. Humans want other humans to do good things to them, therefore, Jesus said that they should do good things to others, as well. Jesus did not limit by which actions people are to treat other people the way they want to be treated, but He said 'in everything' which leaves no exclusion on the action for which to treat people right. This principle is so valuable that it is called 'The Golden Rule' because it is perceived as valuable as gold. The yardstick Jesus wants humans to use in their treatment of other humans is how they would like to be treated by other humans. This is the best yardstick to measure how one should treat another human. "If we say that we have no sin, we are deceiving ourselves and the truth is not in us." (1 John 1:8). Humans are born sinners; therefore, all humans have fallen short of the glory of God. Humans have sinned to God and to their fellow human beings. Humans are all guilty of offending other people, and in a similar manner, others have offended them. However, Jesus expects Christians to forgive other human beings. Christians, to live victorious life must incorporate the acts of forgiveness in their life. Forgiveness builds up relationships, but inability to forgive destroys relationships. Unforgiveness is a self-made prison which locks up those who harbor it and poisons their soul. Unforgiveness is a battle which draws people back from having a fulfilled life. Unforgiveness is toxic to the body just as drugs, alcohol, and any unhealthy habits could poison and destroy the body, gradually, so is the spirit of unforgiveness. Unforgiveness is a pervasive sin which spreads throughout the mind and the body just as cancer destroys its host. An unforgiving spirit suffers from the poison produced in their bodies as the byproducts of unforgiveness increase in their biological system. While they are suffering the consequences of their unforgiveness, the one they refuse to forgive continues to live an abundant life. This means that an unforgiving spirit is its own worst enemy destroying itself. Self-righteousness, hatred, and pride lead to an increased spirit of unforgiveness which is sin, usually directed against the people closest and dearest to the perpetrators of unforgiveness. "Unforgiveness is often a family sin. Husbands won't forgive their wives; wives won't forgive their husbands; children won't forgive their parents and parents won't forgive their children." (Carlin Lawrence). Peter emphasizes the importance regarding the treatment of others in enhancing answered prayers. Peter, in his pieces of advice implies plainly that unforgiveness is an hinderance to answered prayers. "You husbands in the same way, live with *your wives in an understanding way, as with someone weaker, since she is a woman*; and show her honor as a fellow heir of the grace of life, so that your prayers will not be hindered." (1 Peter 3:7). Just as unforgiveness persists among families, friends, and those with close association, so it is among fellow believers. The situation of unforgiveness could be so bad between those who profess to be Christians that although they worship together in the same place, they refuse to talk to each other, separate themselves from each other, and having no close association with each other. Based on Peter's proclamation, it is difficult to pray to God with unkind treatments of each other and expect those prayers to be answered. When people pray and expect the prayers to be answered they should do it with unison of spirit without any form of contention between them. Leaders of any organization or group should make forgiving others their priority and regular practice because their followers could do things which offend them. Pastors should be willing to forgive their church members, and the church members should be willing, as well, to forgive their pastors, realizing that none of them on either side is perfect and that God is still working on each of them and that He is not finished with them. Humans would not get to perfection until they see God out of this world, therefore, they should be will willing to forgive and put up with each other for the good of others as well as for their own good. Paul has a candid piece of advice for the Ephesians regarding how they should treat each other. His pieces of advice zeroed in on their unity and in order for their unity to be strong Paul saw some things in which they had been engaged from which they needed to refrain. Being a witness to how the Ephesians treat each other, Paul was in an ideal position to give them candid pieces of advice not only to improve their responses to each other, but more importantly to improve their relationship with God. Paul pointed out some hinderances to them having good relationship to each other and to God when he said, "Let all bitterness and wrath and anger and clamor and slander be put away from you, along with all malice. Be kind to one another, tender-hearted, forgiving each other, just as God in Christ also has forgiven you. (Ephesians 4:31–32, NASB 1995). Paul discovered that the Colossians were plagued with similar problems as the Ephesians, therefore, he turned his attention to addressing their issues and provided them with some pieces of advice on resolving their issues. "So, as those who have been chosen of God, holy and beloved, put on a heart of compassion, kindness, humility, gentleness, and patience; bearing with one another, and forgiving each other, whoever has a complaint against anyone; just as the Lord forgave you, so must you do also. In addition to all these things, put on love, which is the perfect bond of unity."

(Colossians 3:12–14). Similar pieces of advice which Paul gave to the Ephesians and to the Colossians are equally applicable to all humans today.

Forgiveness is more beneficial to the offended than it is for the one who has committed the offence. Forgiving someone does not erase the offence, but it clears the mind of the offended human beings by following the Lord's direction and confirming that they are fallible and prone to offend others, as well. The offender might not apologize or there might not be opportunity for the offender to apologize based on whatever situation follows the offence, regardless of the situation, all God requires of humans is to forgive those who have done wrong to them. Although, forgiveness does not remove the pain or hardships associated with the offence God expects humans to forgive others. By forgiving others, humans have turned their battles over to God relying on the fact that God would overcome for them and make everything right. With humans, it is impossible by human nature to forgive others, but with God, nothing is impossible and the power or the Holy Spirit could give humans the grace to truly forgive. When humans forgive others, they reap the benefits associated with their spirit of forgiveness rather than the consequences of bitterness of unforgiveness. When humans refuse to forgive those who have offended them, they might be forfeiting the availability of God's forgiveness for them. When humans through their actions of lack of forgiveness deprive themselves of the forgiveness provided by God their sins might not be forgiven, as well. When human sins persist, they block their access to the throne of grace. When their sins persist, their prayers might not be answered and they might be all on their own to face their battles. "But if you do not forgive other people, then your Father will not forgive your offenses. (Matthew 6; 15). Throughout the Scripture, God tells humans how to find His salvation. Humans must be convinced that they need Him. Those who feel self-sufficient will never find salvation in Jesus Christ.

"Forgiveness, in a psychological sense, is the intentional and voluntary process by which one who may feel initially wronged, victimized, harmed, or hurt goes through a process in changing feelings and attitude regarding a given offender for his/her actions, and overcomes the impact of the offense, flaw or mistake including negative emotions such as resentment or a desire for vengeance. Theorists differ in the extent to which they believe forgiveness also implies replacing the negative emotions with positive attitudes (i.e. an increased ability to tolerate the offender), or requires reconciliation with the offender." (Wikipedia). Although the definition above is a secular definition of the word and the actions needed for true forgiveness, it is in line with the way God expects humans to act in forgiving others. Forgiveness is an intentional act. Different people might perceive forgiveness in different ways; however, the end result of forgiveness is an intentional act of letting go resentment and anger. When the offended let go of the hurt, they obtain the freedom not to be handicapped by the feelings or the hurt caused by the offence. When humans forgive each other, they are no longer held down by the bondage of the hurt or anger against the offending human being. They could easily approach God with a clean mind and request assistance from God to fight their battles. Forgiveness is the act of pardoning an offender. Forgiveness in Greek has the connotation of 'letting go' which implies to letting a debt go when the debtor is unable to pay. In the same manner when an offence has been committed there is little that an offender could do to erase the effects of the offence. In the case of debt when it is obvious that the debtor is unable to pay, the creditor is to let go the debt which in the present time is called debt forgiveness. When humans forgive others, they let go of resentment and abandon any claim to be compensated for the hurt or loss they have suffered, in that situation, it could be called 'offence forgiveness.' Humans are born sinners, they are not able to pay for their inborn sins, but God was gracious by sending His Son, Jesus Christ to the world to let go the sins of humanity. God at that time did and does no longer count human sins against them. Then God employ humans to replicate His forgiveness to their fellow human beings. "Bearing with one another, and forgiving each other, whoever has a complaint against anyone; just as the Lord forgave you, so must you do also." (Colossians 3:13). God was not asking humans to do something He has not done, first. God wants humans to be His ambassadors to the world and to each other by extending their forgiveness to others as God has extended forgiveness to humans through the death of Christ on the cross for all to have eternal life. Without God's forgiveness no one could survive His wrath for all the offenses committed against Him. God does not want humans to count the number of offenses other humans have committed against them and the number of times they have forgiven them, but to forgive them every time as if it is the first time. Jesus made this concept clear in His discus with Peter. "Then Peter came up and said to Him, "Lord, how many times shall my brother sin against me and I still forgive him? Up to seven times?" Jesus said to him, "I do not say to you, up to seven times, but up to seventy-seven times." (Matthew 18:21–22). In this discuss, Jesus let Peter know that there was no reason to be counting offences and the frequency of the forgiveness, but to forgive each time an offence occurs. God does not count how many times humans have sinned against Him and how many times He has forgiven them, but He forgives and has made provision for the forgiveness of sins every time one is committed against Him, through the blood of Jesus Christ. The hinderance to human forgiveness of their sins against God is their reluctance to go to Christ for the forgiveness of their sins. Humans have the battle of not acknowledging God, their redeemer, and their battles persist until they move to God to fight their battles for them. Humans are encouraged to obey the words of God and one of the words of God is to forgive those who have wrongly treated them. Therefore, forgiving others is the act of being obedient to God. Resentment is an impediment to human health. When humans do not forgive, they are not only disobeying God, but they are in the process of destroying their own health, gradually. In other words, when humans do not forgive others, they are harboring unhealthy emotions which hurt them relatively more than the ones against whom they are holding grudges. As humans abandon unforgiveness and various bitterness and anger accompanying them, they are freed to serve, live in real peace, joy, and develop into spiritual maturity. In humans' own strength, forgiving others in the way they have received from God is impossible, however, with God, nothing is impossible, and with His Spirit inside humans they can work on the steps which leads to true forgiveness.

Holding grudges and hurting oneself is a battle which only God could assist humans to overcome, however, the assistance could happen only by submitting to the will of God and inviting Him for assistance to win that battle. Only God has the power to undo the roots of bitterness which appears to fester in the minds of individuals thus causing troubles and defiling others. "See to it that no one comes short of the grace of God; that no root of bitterness springing up causes trouble, and by it many become defiled; (Hebrews 12:15). If you have a situation for which you have made up your mind that you could never forgive the one who has done wrong to you, but by taking it to God in prayers He is able to give you the grace to forgive the one who has done wrong to you. Your battle is the determination or the making up of your mind not to forgive, but by taking it to God in prayers He will soften your heart to forgive those who have done you wrong. Your battle will be over, and you will be able to live in peace to enjoy the rest of your existence. Generally, humans can tolerate other people as long as they are doing things in a way which is pleasing to them. However, such tolerance could be temporary, because immediately they do things differently from the way they prefer and to which they are accustomed, humans could easily change their composure. Humans could easily change their allegiance and support once things are not going the way they like and begin their critical nature. Humans, generally, have selective bad memories remembering the good done for them, previously, but they dwell on what is being done for them in the moment. Many humans do not have it in them to give allowance for the shortcomings of others, but they prefer to stand in the judgement seats to condemn others. However, humans need to be tolerant of others, realizing that they are not perfect themselves and as a result, they should extend allowances and grace to other human beings. It is, therefore, important for humans to be fully aware that people are not perfect and just as others could fall short of their expectations so could they fall short of others' expectations of them, as well. When humans have such type of expectations it would be easier to give others allowance as they would want others to give them. "Simon, Simon, behold, Satan has demanded to sift you like wheat; but I have prayed for you, that your faith will not fail; and you, when you have turned back, strengthen your brothers." (Luke 22:31–32). Jesus set a great example in His dealings with Simon Peter.

Simon Peter was one of the closest trusted disciples to Jesus. If one would be sure of someone who would not deny Jesus under any circumstance, the first disciple to be mentioned would be Simon Peter. Simon Peter himself was very sure of nothing to make him deny Jesus that he said it directly to Jesus. In fact, Simon Peter was so ready to defend Jesus that he cut off a servant's ear when Jesus was being arrested. Jesus appreciated the devotion of Simon Peter to Him, but He knew that Simon Peter would eventually deny Him. Jesus was not resentful that Simon Peter would deny Him when the situation got precarious, but He started praying for Simon Peter. Jesus did not hold grudge about Simon Peter disappointing and denying Him when the situation got very tough, but Jesus started praying for Simon Peter. This was a great example which Jesus set for all humans. The example is for people to pray for those who have disappointed them one way or the other instead of holding grudges. When humans truthfully pray for those who have disappointed or mistreated them, they could not be holding grudges against them. People need to move to God to assist them to conquer the battle of unforgiveness. When humans see the failings of their brother, the love they have for them should lead them to make allowance for them and when it is necessary, they let them know the truth in a loving manner. Jesus understood the situation which made Simon Peter deny Him, not once, but three times. Jesus was ready to restore Simon Peter to His service without holding any grudge against him or condemning him. Whenever humans have offended each other, they should pray to God to make amends and restore the relationships. The human tendency is to hold on to hurt feelings without giving allowances for other humans' mistakes. Humans have the propensity not to forgive others when they hold on to hurt feelings which increases resentments. They have all turned aside, together they are corrupt; There is no one who does good, not even one. (Psalm 14:3). Here the Psalmist declares that everyone is a sinner, no one is perfect, therefore, humans should learn to make allowance for other human beings when they act imperfectly instead of berating or hating them. When humans do not give allowance to the shortcomings of others, they behave like hypocrites because they are not any better than those with shortcomings. " You hypocrite, first take the log out of your own eye, and then you will see clearly to take the]speck out of your brother's eye!' (Matthew 7:5). Humans need to move to God and pray to Him to remove the battle of critical spirit far away from them and replace it with the spirit of forgiveness. God is the God of love and the God of grace Who wants humans to imitate Him in their dealings with other human beings. Humans with critical attitudes never show grace and are not gracious, even for what God has done for them. They have the tendency to put other people down instead of lifting them up, they tend to be critical instead of being understanding, they tend to revenge instead of showing forgiveness, and they never forget the wrong that was ever done to them by others, but they keep them on top of their minds with the intention to strike back whenever opportunities to do so present themselves. The importance of humans making allowance for others is to extend the grace they receive from God to others. God is always gracious to humans; therefore, they should extend similar grace to others. It might not be easy to replicate similar grace to certain human beings for what they might have done, however, when humans realize that they are not perfect themselves they will be able to muster the courage to replicate what God has done for them to others. He even sent His one and only son to die on the cross for our sins. Paul realized that, at times, dealing with human beings could be challenging, therefore, he admonished the Ephesians to show humility, gentleness, patience seasoned with love in dealing with other human beings. This admonition by Paul was not easy to carry out when dealing with humans, however, with humans it is impossible, but with God it is possible. Therefore, humans need to move to God to solve the battles of unforgiveness, impatience, holding grudges, and lack of love in order to see other human beings as God sees them. "… with all humility and gentleness, with patience, bearing with one another in love," (Ephesians 4:2b). When humans make allowance for other human's shortcomings, they are responding appropriately as someone who has been forgiven by Jesus and one who has been washed by His blood and is ready to extend to other humans the forgiveness the Lord has granted them. They need to pray to God to give them the patience to deal with other human beings, gently, and making allowance for each other's faults because of the love of God which binds them.

How Should You Fight Your Battle?

There are many ways by which humans fight their battles, however, there are the right and the wrong ways to fight battles. The wrong ways to fight battles are not exhaustive by the following examples. Humans fight their battle by relying on their own ability, by relying on the ability and loyalty of others, by turning to other unhealthy habits; all those ways of fighting human battles are short sighted and they mostly lead to failures. Some people have gotten involved with harmful wrong companies in order to fight their battles, but instead of getting relief they run into bigger troubles and into untenable issues. Some people get themselves into drugs or other evil vices which do not lessen their troubles but increase their headaches. As it is evident that the first option to fight one's battle is a failure when humans make attempts, in their own power. Therefore, a better option is to allow God to fight the battle for humans. Because what appears to humans as an effective way and strategy to fight human battles without God in charge ends up in futility.

"There is a way which seems right to a person, but its end is the way of death. Even in laughter the heart may be in pain, And the end of joy may be grief." (Proverbs 14:12–13). Based on the principle that God should be invited and allowed to fight human battle, how do you fight your battle? Could you declare as the lyrics of the song below state how you fight your battle? If you are not able to confidently say how you fight your battle with the involvement of God, today is the day of salvation to get God involved in fighting your battles. Try God and you will see the difference in your winnings and in your peace of mind regardless of whatever happens. You are not surrounded by your battles only, but you are surrounded by God's success and peace, therefore, do not be faint hearted when the battles are raging and there seem to be no end to the upheavals.

"This is how I fight my battles

(There's a table)

This is how I fight my battles
This is how I fight my battles
This is how I fight my battles

This is how I fight my battles
This is how I fight my battles
This is how I fight my battles.

It may look like I'm surrounded, but I'm surrounded by You
It may look like I'm surrounded, but I'm surrounded by You
It may look like I'm surrounded, but I'm surrounded by You
It may look like I'm surrounded, but I'm surrounded by You.

This is how I fight my battles
This is how I fight my battles
This is how I fight my battles
This is how I fight my battles.

This is how I fight my battles
This is how I fight my battles
This is how I fight my battles

At Your table.
It may look like I'm surrounded, but I'm surrounded by You
It may look like I'm surrounded, but I'm surrounded by You

Dr. David Ajeigbe

It may look like I'm surrounded, but I'm surrounded by You
It may look like I'm surrounded, but I'm surrounded by You.

This is how I fight my battles
This is how I fight my battles
This is how I fight my battles

This is how I

This is how I fight my battles
 This is how I fight my battles
This is how I fight my battles

It may look like

It may look like I'm surrounded, but I'm surrounded by You
It may look like I'm surrounded, but I'm surrounded by You
It may look like I'm surrounded, but I'm surrounded by You
It may look like I'm surrounded, but I'm surrounded by You.

Nothing is as strong as Your blood
Nothing is as strong as Your blood
Nothing is as strong as Your blood
Nothing is as strong as Your blood.

This is how I fight my battles
Right here at Your table
Your blood and Your body has overcome
Your blood and Your body has overcome.

It may look like I'm surrounded, but I'm surrounded by You
It may look like I'm surrounded, but I'm surrounded by You
It may look like I'm surrounded, but I'm surrounded by You
It may look like I'm surrounded, but I'm surrounded by You.
This is how I fight my battles
This is how I fight my battles
This is how I fight my battles

How Do You Fight Your Battle?!!!

This is how,

This is how we fight our battles
This is how we fight our battles.

You've already overcome
You have already overcome
You have already overcome
Oh, this is how I fight my battles.

This is how I fight my battles
Grace, grace, grace
This is how I fight my battles
Oh, this is how I fight my battles
Grace.

It may look like I'm surrounded, but I'm surrounded by You
It may look like I'm surrounded."
(Elyssa Smith/Alyssa Smith).

"Then we turned and went up the road to Bashan, and Og, king of Bashan, came out with all his people to meet us in battle at Edrei. But the Lord said to me, 'Do not fear him, for I have handed him and all his people and his land over to you; and you shall do to him just as you did to Sihon king of the Amorites, who lived in Heshbon'" (Deuteronomy 3:1–3).

When troubles come and the battles rage on, it is easy to lose focus on who is able to help humans overcome their troubles. As a result, humans look for alternative ways to resolve their issues on their own power instead of relying on the power of God. The Bible states that" No temptation has overtaken you except something common to mankind; and God is faithful, so He will not allow you to be tempted beyond what you are able, but with the temptation will provide the way of escape also, so that you will be able to endure it." (1 Corinthians 10:13). When battles are raging for humans, God is not far, but close to provide victory for every individual going through hardship. All God expects of humans is to trust Him that He is able to give them victory over their battles. When humans rely on God their battles become God's battles and He will send His army to fight human battles. God is human's armor, shield, defense, and shelter in time of trouble. Some battles linger, even with steadfast prayers and trust in God, on such occasions humans should believe that the will of God will overcome. Humans might wonder how the hardships and difficulties they are dealing with could be the will of God for them. Humans could be wondering whether they could ever win their battles. On such occasions, humans should trust God with the believe that God would never abandon them and although they do not know the future, they should have their hope set on God. God would give them grace to endure and win their battles. With the hope in God, humans would realize that what appear to be insurmountable mountains would be turned to level grounds. The Psalmist said it profoundly;

> "God is our refuge and strength,
> A very ready help in trouble.
> Therefore we will not fear, though the earth shakes
> And the mountains slip into the heart of the sea;
> Though its waters roar and foam,
> Though the mountains quake at its swelling pride. Selah
> "There is a river whose streams make the city of God happy,
> The holy dwelling places of the Most High.
> God is in the midst of her, she will not be moved;
> God will help her [c]when morning dawns.
> The nations made an uproar, the kingdoms tottered;
> He raised His voice, the earth quaked.
> The LORD of armies is with us;

The God of Jacob is our stronghold." (Psalm 46:1–7). God is always ready to help humans out of their predicaments and battles, God expects humans to move close to Him and seek His assistance. God is human refuge, strength, and He is always present to fight human battles. Just like a chicken protects her chicks under her wings so the Lord protects humans under His wings. Just as the chicks run under the wings of the hen should humans run under the protection of God. God is aware of human sufferings, hardships, troubles and wars and He is ever ready to save humans from their mounting battles. God is ever present and, on the set, to spring up into action to rescue humans from their predicaments.

"You are not hidden
There's never been a moment
You were forgotten
You are not hopeless
Though you have been broken
Your innocence stolen

I hear you whisper underneath your breath
I hear your SOS, your SOS
I will send out an army to find you
In the middle of the darkest night
It's true, I will rescue you

There is no distance
That cannot be covered
Over and over
You're not defenseless
I'll be your shelter
I'll be your armor

I hear you whisper underneath your breath
I hear your SOS, your SOS

I will send out an army to find you
In the middle of the darkest night
It's true, I will rescue you
I will never stop marching to reach you
In the middle of the hardest fight
It's true, I will rescue you

I hear the whisper underneath your breath
I hear you whisper, you have nothing left

I will send out an army to find you
In the middle of the darkest night

It's true, I will rescue you
I will never stop marching to reach you
In the middle of the hardest fight
It's true, I will rescue you
Oh, I will rescue you."
(Lauren Daigle).

God is ever ready to rescue human beings and to give them victory when all hope is gone. It is when human ability is no longer adequate and they are no longer able to carry on and are close to giving up all efforts that God comes for the rescue. What then shall we say to these things? If God is for us, who is against us? He who did not spare His own Son, but delivered Him over for us all, how will He not also with Him freely give us all things? Who will bring charges against God's elect? God is the one who justifies; who is the one who condemns? Christ Jesus is He who died, but rather, was raised, who is at the right hand of God, who also intercedes for us. Who will separate us from the love of Christ? Will tribulation, trouble, or persecution, or famine, or nakedness, or danger, or sword? Just as it is written:

For Your sake we are killed all day long;
We were regarded as sheep to be slaughtered

But in all these things we overwhelmingly conquer through Him who loved us. For I am convinced that neither death, nor life, nor angels, nor principalities, nor things present, nor things to come, nor powers, nor height, nor depth, nor any other created thing will be able to separate us from the love of God that is in Christ Jesus our Lord." (Romans 8:31–39). Through the struggles of life humans should not allow any of them to separate them from the love of God. The love of God for His creatures is endless. God is always creating opportunities to aide His creatures. When the road appears long and lonely, God is directing human paths. Humans just need to follow God's directions as He directs and not deviate from His leading. God always has His sleeves rolled up in preparation to step into the fight on behalf of His creatures. All God expects of His creatures is for them not to despair, not to give up, and not to abandon their hope in Him because their Savior is ready to take up their battles. Give your battles to Him because He is able to fight and win them for you.

> "…. I need the kinda love that can outlast the night
> I need the kinda love that is willing to fight
>
> … When the going gets tough
> And my strength's not enough
> I see You showing up like never before
> This battle for my heart
> You took on from the start
> You are the peace when my mind's at war
> And oh
>
> … You will never stop fighting for me
> When I can't fight for myself
> Every word is a promise You keep
> 'Cause You love me like nobody else
> You stand up for me in the darkest night
> When my faith is weak You're still by my side
> You will never stop fighting for me
> You will never stop fighting for me
>
> … In the perfect timing You make all things right
> You paint a silver lining in this heart of mine
>
> … When the going gets tough
> And my strength's not enough
> I see You showing up like never before
> This battle for my heart
> You took on from the start
> You are the peace when my mind's at war
> And oh
>
> … You will never stop fighting for me
> When I can't fight for myself
> Every word is a promise You keep
> 'Cause You love me like nobody else
> You stand up for me in the darkest night
> When my faith is weak You're still by my side

You will never stop fighting for me
You will never stop fighting for me

... Your love
 Is winning me over
Your heart
Is pulling me closer
Your love
Is winning me over
Your heart
Is pulling me closer

... You will never stop
Fighting for me, fighting for me
Every word is a promise You keep
Ohh, yeah

... You will never stop fighting for me
When I can't fight for myself (when I can't)
Every word is a promise You keep (ohh)
'Cause You love me like nobody else
You stand up for me in the darkest night (You stand up for me in the dark)
When my faith is weak You're still by my side (yeah, yeah, my side)
You will never stop fighting for me
You will never stop fighting for me."
Ethan Hulse/Jordan Sapp/Riley Clemmons.

    At times, in the middle of the battles of life there is the tendency to want to give up and let it all go. Humans could easily get exhausted with the battles which persist. It might appear as if there could never be the light at the end of the tunnel. The tunnel might appear endless in the middle of all upheavals. It is at those times when humans are ready to give up all hopes that God is ready to renew their hopes. Humans are to be courageous and endure the hardship of the moment because God will surely come to their rescue. David was a man who experienced troubles and the ups and downs of life, victories, and losses. David lived a life as a fugitive in exile, upheavals, insecurity, and uncertainty. However, with his troubles and shortcomings he trusted God and he was pronounced by God as a man after God's heart. (Acts 13:22). When there appeared to be no 'light at the end of the tunnel' for David, he called upon the Lord in frustration; but when his condition improved, he raised his voice to praise the Lord. In all his ups and downs, David stayed with the Lord and he remained faithful. In good times, in bad times, and in the times in between, David did not allow his situation to be in his way of being devoted to the Lord. David emphasized endurance and patience with the present difficulties of life because of the belief that God will bring victory. Although there is sadness or unhappiness with the present human situation God would bring about a joyful ending very soon. With this saying David was implying that humans need to be patient and give God a chance to fight and win their battles.

> "I will exalt You, Lord, for You have lifted me up, And have not let my enemies rejoice over me. Lord my God, I cried to You for help, and You healed me. Lord, You have brought up my soul from Sheol; You have kept me alive,]that I would not go down to the pit. Sing praise to the Lord, you His godly ones, And praise the mention of His holiness. For His anger is but for a moment, His favor is for a lifetime; Weeping may last for the night, But a shout of joy comes in the morning." (Psalm 30:1–3).

After David's lifetime experiences with heartaches and godly favor, he wrote, using his firsthand experiences with pain, anxiety, and struggles of life to encourage humas that their present situations are temporary and that God's lasting joy lies around the corner. David called out to the Lord, in his darkest time and God answered him. This should serve as an encouragement to humans to call on the Lord in their difficult times because His ears are opened to their cry and He will answer them steadily.

It is important for humans to know that any night does not last forever, but the sun will always rise, and at daybreak, the blessing and favor of the God will come. God is hard at work to strengthen, deliver, and bless humans. Even for the most faithful followers of God, life poses its painful struggles with imperfections and hardships, however, in the midst of those struggles, God is with humans constantly and working the good out of their lives.

Jeremiah, the prophet, wrote, "blessed are those who trust in the Lord and have made the Lord their hope and confidence. They are like trees planted along a riverbank, with roots that reach deep into the water. Such trees are not bothered by the heat or worried by long months of drought. Their leaves stay green, and they never stop producing fruit." (Jeremiah 17:7–8). The words of Jeremiah are very encouraging by giving the assurance that God will make everything new and that God will turn the difficulties of the present to future blessing and the sadness of today into abundant joy in the future. However, when humans look at their situations, they might wonder how those words could come to life for them. When humans have such thoughts roaming around their minds it become difficult to approach God to fight their battles and their anxiety and unbelief increase. It is at that time that humans need to yield to the words of Paul in his pieces of advice to the Philippians when he said, "Do not be anxious about anything, but in everything by prayer and pleading with thanksgiving let your requests be made known to God. And the peace of God, which surpasses all comprehension, will guard your hearts and minds in Christ Jesus." (Philippians 4:6–7). In times of despair, humans should go to God with prayers and supplications and 'pour out their hearts' to Him. God's ears are attentive to the cry of His children, and He would surely deliver those who have called unto Him. Jonah testified to this fact when he said,

> "But you have brought up my life from the pit, O Lord my God. While I was fainting away, I remembered the Lord, and my prayer came to You, into Your holy temple." (Jonah 2:7).

Humans should be confident that God will fight their battles and give them victory over their adversaries, as long as they put their trust in Him. At times doubts could creep into human minds as to whether God has forgotten then and whether He would come to their help in their battles and in their hardships. However, humans should take courage that God will not forget them, and He is powerful to win their battles in due time if they do not lose heart. The Israelites, in their troubles doubted the care of God for them, thinking that the Lord had forgotten them in their problems. However, God responded through prophet Isaiah thus, "Do you not know? Have you not heard? The Everlasting God, the Lord, the Creator of the ends of the earth. Does not become weary or tired. His understanding is inscrutable. He gives strength to the weary, and to him who lacks might He increases power. Though youths grow weary and tired, and vigorous young men stumble badly, yet those who wait for the Lord will gain new strength; they will mount up with wings like eagles, they will run and not get tired, they will walk and not become weary." (Isaiah 4:28–31). God wanted the Israelites to know that He is in control, He had great plans for them which they might not understand yet, but He would manifest to them in due time. God wanted them to know that he did not forget them and that he would give them what they needed to be victorious. Whenever humans are doubting the will of God for them, they should know that God has them in His mind. God is all powerful and he has a plan, and that plan is ultimately good.

"For I know the plans I have for you," declares the Lord, "plans to prosper you and not to harm you, plans to give you hope and a future." (Jeremiah 29:11). When humans begin to think that God does not care for them in their battles they should remember the teaching of Jesus about how much significance God gives to humans than other one of His creatures. "Are not two sparrows sold for a copper coin? And not one of them falls to the ground apart from your Father's will. But the very hairs of your head are all numbered. Do not fear, therefore; you are of more value than many sparrows." (Matthew 10:29–31, NKJV). Jesus was saying that two sparrows combined are very small and insignificant, but God, their creator cares for them. Jesus was pointing out to humans that they are more significant than two sparrows. Therefore, the fact that God cares for the two sparrows is an indication that humans should not worry because God cares much more for them. Humans are to put their trust in God with the confidence that God will hold on to them in their battles.

"When the best of me is barely breathing'
When I'm not somebody I believe in
Hold on to me
When I miss the light the night has stolen
When I'm slammin' all the doors You've opened
Hold on to me
Hold on to me

Hold on to me when it's too dark to see You
When I am sure I have reached the end
Hold on to me when I forget I need You
When I let go, hold me again
When I don't feel like I'm worth defending
When I'm tired of all my pretending
Hold on to me

When I start to break in desperation
Underneath the weight of expectation
Hold on to me
Hold on to me
Hold on to me when it's too dark to see You (I'll hold on)
When I am sure I have reached the end
Hold on to me when I forget I need You (I'll hold on)
When I let go, hold me again I could rest here in Your arms forever
'Cause I know nobody loves me better Hold on to me Hold on to me."
(Paul Mabury/Paul Duncan/Lauren Daigle).

"Soon afterward Jesus went to a city called Nain; and His disciples were going along with Him, accompanied by a large crowd. Now as He approached the gate of the city, a dead man was being carried out, the only son of his mother, and she was a widow; and a sizeable crowd from the city was with her. When the Lord saw her, He felt compassion for her and said to her, "Do not go on weeping." And He came up and touched the coffin; and the bearers came to a halt. And He said, "Young man, I say to you, arise!" And the dead man sat up and began to speak. And Jesus gave him back to his mother. Fear gripped them all, and they began glorifying God, saying, "A great prophet has appeared among us!" and, "God has visited His people!" (Luke 7:11–16). The widow had no husband to provide for her needs and the only son she had providing for her needs died. The death of her son must have been very devastating to her. The woman must have been too old to bear another child and even if she wanted to try, she had no husband. Even if she was able to have another child, the child would have been too young to be of any assistance to her. The widow was in a precarious position, and she might have been wondering what would become of her. Looking at the woman's face Jesus must have seen the grief on her face with the battle of loneliness which had just happened to her. Jesus condoled the woman and had compassion on her. Jesus was present at the right time to comfort the woman and to do for her what no other person in the congregation could do for her. When humans have lost all hope and they are confused and bewildered about the next step to take to get out of their battles, a meeting with Jesus could resolve their battles, instantaneously. Jesus saved the woman from her disgrace, grief, and an upcoming loneliness and lack of provision for her needs.

On another occasion, Jesus raised Jairus daughter who was dead. "And one of the synagogue officials, named Jairus, came, and upon seeing Him, fell at His feet and pleaded with Him earnestly, saying, "My little daughter is at the point of death; please come and lay Your hands on her, so that she will get well and live." And He went off with him; and a large crowd was following Him and pressing in on Him. A woman who had had a hemorrhage for twelve years and had endured much at the hands of many physicians and had spent all that she had and was not helped at all, but instead had become worse— after hearing about Jesus, she came up in the crowd behind Him and touched His cloak. For she had been saying to herself, "If I just touch His garments, I will get well. "And immediately the flow of her blood was dried up; and she felt in her body that she was healed of her disease. And immediately Jesus, perceiving in Himself that power from Him had gone out, turned around in the crowd and said, "Who touched My garments?" And His disciples said to Him, "You see the crowd pressing in on You, and You say, 'Who touched Me?'" And He looked around to see the woman who had done this. But the woman, fearing and trembling, aware of what had happened to her, came and fell down before Him and told Him the whole truth. And He said to her, "Daughter, your faith has made you well; go in peace and be cured of your disease. "While He was still speaking, people came from the house of the synagogue official, saying, "Your daughter has died; why bother the Teacher further?" But Jesus, overhearing what was being spoken, said to the synagogue official, "Do not be afraid, only believe." And He allowed no one to accompany Him except Peter, James, and John the brother of James. They came to the house of the synagogue official, and He saw a commotion, and people loudly weeping and wailing. And after entering, He said to them, "Why are you making a commotion and weeping? The child has not died but is asleep." And they *began* laughing at Him. But putting them all outside, He took along the child's father and mother and His own companions, and entered the room where the child was in bed. And taking the child by the hand, He said to her, "Talitha, kum!" (Which translated means, "Little girl, I say to you, get up!"). And immediately the girl got up and began to walk, for she was twelve years old. And immediately they were completely astonished. And He gave them strict orders that no one was to know about this, and He told them to have something given her to eat." (Mark 5:21–43).

Jesus took time off his busy schedule to attend to the needs of Jairus. Jairus pleaded to Jesus to heal his daughter who was sick and on the point of death. At that point Jesus abandoned His schedule and headed to Jairus home to heal her daughter. However, on His way He was hijacked by another woman who has been fighting her issue of bleeding for a while. This woman had done all that was humanly possible, but nothing worked for her. The woman took advantage of Jesus being around and she moved closer to Jesus to win the battle of her unbated bleeding.

Jesus proved His ability to multi-task when the need arose or arises. In attending to the issues around the woman, Jesus was late to prevent Jairus daughter from dying. However, Jesus was and is in control of human life and human affairs whether the human is dead or alive. All Jesus needed or needs to win human battles is for human to go to Him and hand their battles over to Him. The woman with the battle of blood handed all to Jesus and she was cured. Jairus daughter died before Jesus got to Jairus house, but her death did not stop Jesus from winning the battle of death for her. The arrival of Jesus brought the return of life to the lifeless daughter.

Everyone was amazed and praised God. God got the glory as Jesus won the battles for those who were afflicted. If you are afflicted with different kinds of battles in your life, take them Jesus who is more than able to win your battles satisfactorily.

In another occasion Jesus brought Lazarus, His family friend back to life. Lazarus had been dead for few days and he had been buried and everyone thought that all hope was over before Jesus showed up. In fact, Lazarus' sisters were persuading Jesus not to bother to have the grave opened because they were sure that the decaying process of Lazarus body had started and by opening the grave it would expose everyone present to the terrible smell of Lazarus' decaying body. They had all given up hope. However, Jesus was persistent that the grave be opened. Upon opening the grave, Jesus called Lazarus to come out and Lazarus listened to Jesus and came out. All the thoughts of those present were proved to be unfounded because Jesus won the battle of death and decay for Lazarus. Everyone present marveled. If you have battles you are fighting, do not give up and throw your hands in the air, but take your battles to Jesus and He will win your battles for you. Only trust and obey Him. Do whatever Jesus tells you to do and all will be well. At the grave of Lazarus, Jesus was being persuaded not to open the grave of Lazarus, but upon Jesus' insistence they obeyed Him and all was well. When Jesus declared that Lazarus was just asleep and not dead, He was reviving the hopes of those present including Lazarus' sisters. Jesus is the hope of those who have died and those who are alive. Jesus proved that He could bring those who have died back into life. Jesus could win the battles for those who put their hope in Him regardless of whatever has happened. All will be well with you once you obey Jesus and follow His directives (John 11:1–44). Hope is like a ray of light through the thick cloud; therefore, humans should always keep their hope in Christ alive because He will break through for them all the time. Keep hope alive!

Humans need to know that, although they might not win all their battles in this world, they need to be assured that their victory is waiting for them in heaven where no one could deprive them of it. In heaven their victory has been sealed by the blood of Christ which was shed for them on the cross in Calvary. Praying, putting ones' trust in God and still feeling that ones' prayers are not being answered is not God's abandonment of human beings, but on the other side it might be the fulfilment of God's will and purpose for human life. An example of this could be seen when Jesus was praying for the cup to pass over Him. In the same prayer Jesus pointed out that it should not be based on what He wanted, but God's will was supreme to His. "Then Jesus came with them to a place called Gethsemane, and told His disciples, sit here while I go over there and pray. And He took Peter and the two sons of Zebedee with Him and He began to be distressed. Then He said to them, My soul is deeply grieved, to the point of death; remain here and keep watch with Me. And He went a little beyond them, and fell on His face and prayed, saying, My Father, if it is possible, let this cup pass from Me; yet not as I will, but as You will." (Matthew 26:36–39).

Humans need to realize that in order to get completed they need to submit their will to the supreme will of God. With such submission God's glory will shine in human life and they will reap the full benefits of the battle the Lord has taken over on their behalf. Human winning is temporary and not satisfying without the assistance from God. Human victory is not long lasting and it could be stopped, but when the victory emanated from God, no one can stop the Lord Almighty.

How Do You Fight Your Battle?!!!

As a lamb, Jesus is gentle, kind, and humble, but as a lion Jesus is strong and powerful to protect His own. Therefore, all that humans need to do is to give Jesus homage and bow down before Him. Jesus is ever ready to protect humans as soon as humans get Him involved in their struggles, affairs, and battles. Fighting battles and losing is not due to lack of concerns for humans by God, but it might be as a result of not getting God involved by humans.

"Who Can Stop the Lord Almighty?

He's coming on the clouds.
He's coming on the clouds
Kings and kingdoms will bow down
And every chain will break
As broken hearts declare His praise
For who can stop the Lord Almighty

And our God is the lion
The Lion of Judah
He's roaring with power
And fighting our battles
And every knee will bow before Him
Our God is the lamb
The lamb that was slain
For the sins of the world
His blood breaks the chains
And every knee will bow before the lion and the lamb
Every knee will bow before Him (yeah)

So, open up the gates.

So, open up the gates
Make way before the King of Kings
The God who comes to save
Is here to set the captives free
For who can stop the Lord Almighty

Our God is the lion
The Lion of Judah

Dr. David Ajeigbe

He's roaring with power
And fighting our battles
And every knee will bow before Him
Our God is the lamb
The lamb that was slain
For the sin of the world
His blood breaks the chains
And every knee will bow before the lion and the lamb
Every knee will bow before Him.
"How many here believe
Every knee will bow
Every tongue will confess
And then."

For who can stop the Lord Almighty
Who can stop the Lord Almighty
Who can stop the Lord Almighty
No one
Who can stop
Sing it over the battle?

Yeah, that's it.

Who can stop the Lord Almighty
There is no one
Who can stop the Lord Almighty
Who can stop the Lord (yeah)

And our God is the lion
The Lion of Judah
He's roaring with power
And fighting our battles
And every knee will bow before Him
Our God is the lamb
The lamb that was slain
For the sins of the world
His blood breaks the chains
And every knee will bow before the lion and the lamb
Every knee will bow before Him (yeah)

Every knee will bow
Tongue confesses."
(Brenton Brown/Brian Mark Johnson/Iceland Mooring).

It is said that 'without a test there is no testimony.' "As *Jesus* passed by, He saw a man who had been blind from birth. And His disciples asked Him, Rabbi, who sinned, this man or his parents, that he would be born blind? Jesus answered, it *was* neither that this man sinned nor his parents; but it was so that the works of God might be displayed in him." (John 9:1–3). Humans might feel guilty or might be made to feel guilty when humans are going through some battles. Other people might associate another person's battle with a result of sin. This might be true in some instances, but that is not always true on all occasions. The example of Job could come to mind, quickly (Job 1–3). Job went through his battles which were mistaken by his friends as a result of Job's sins. That assumption was wrong because Job's battles came as a result of his devotion to God and not because of his sins. Therefore, humans are to be careful because when other humans are going through their battles, they do not assume that their battles are results of their sins. Humans are to remain humble regarding other human's battles and not display a 'holier than thou attitude' so as not to be debased, just as Job's friends were. Humans, especially, Christians are to come close to anyone fighting any battle and assist them in their fight without assigning blame. The Bible warned all about proving to be righteous when dealing with other human beings who are fighting any kind of battles. "*Brothers and sisters*, even if a person is caught in any wrongdoing, you who are spiritual are to restore such a person in a spirit of gentleness; each one looking to yourself, so that you are not tempted as well. Bear one another's burdens, and thereby fulfill the law of Christ. For if anyone thinks that he is something when he is nothing, he deceives himself. But each one must examine his own work, and then he will have reason for boasting, but to himself alone, and not to another. For each one will bear his own load. (Galatians 6:1–5B). "Hence, let the one who thinks he stands watch out that he does not fall." 1 Corinthians 10:13 SB).

Dr. David Ajeigbe

You must

You must think I'm strong
To give me what I'm going through
Well, forgive me

… Forgive me if I'm wrong
But this looks like more than I can do
On my own

… I know I'm not strong enough to be
Everything that I'm supposed to be
I give up
I'm not strong enough.

… Hands of mercy won't you cover me
Lord right now I'm asking you to be
Strong enough
Strong enough

… For the both of us, yeah
… Well, maybe
Maybe that's the point

… To reach the point of giving up
'Cause when I'm finally
Finally at rock bottom.

… Well, that's when I start lookin' up
And reachin' out
I know I'm not strong enough to be
Everything that I'm supposed to be

… I give up
I'm not strong enough
Hands of mercy won't you cover me?
Lord right now I'm asking you to be

… Strong enough
Strong enough
'Cause I'm broken
Down to nothing

… But I'm still holding on to the one thing
You are God
And you are strong

… When I am weak
I can do all things
Through Christ who gives me strength
And I don't have to be
Strong enough
Strong enough

… I know I can do all things
Through Christ who gives me strength
And I don't have to be
Strong enough
Strong enough...
Oh...
Yeah...

… I know I'm not strong enough to be
Everything that I'm supposed to be
I give up
I'm not strong enough
Hands of mercy won't you cover me
Lord right now I'm asking you to be
Strong enough
Strong enough
Strong enough."
(Matthew Joseph West).

Humans are not able by themselves to solve their own problems or to fight their battle but their trust in God could take them through any battle or difficulties to a successful end. Humans are impatient and get frustrated when the battle rages on with no end in sight. However, what humans need to do is to give all to God and not to worry about their problems any longer once they have laid them at the feet of Jesus. Issues which humans face do not start in one day, but gradually, therefore, humans should know that although it might end in one day it is all according to the will of God and to His glory. Therefore, humans should be patient when there are no quick fixes as they expect when they pray to God. The initial step for humans is to run fast to God in faith and in deep reliance on Him. It is often said that the journey of a thousand steps starts with the first step, therefore, humans should go to God as their first step in fighting their battles. If humans pray to God and their battles appear to be raging it is important to remember the believers of God in the Bible who prayed to God and it appeared that their prayers were ignored by God. It is important to examine how those believers continue to rely on God and believed that God knows the best and that regardless of whatever happened the Lord is on their side. Paul was one of the great examples for the seemingly unanswered prayers in fighting his battle. "Because of the extraordinary greatness of the revelations, for this reason, to keep me from exalting myself, there was given to me a thorn in the flesh, a messenger of Satan to torment me—to keep me from exalting myself! Concerning this I pleaded with the Lord three times that it might leave me. And He has said to me, My grace is sufficient for you, for power is perfected in weakness. Most gladly, therefore, I will rather boast about my weaknesses, so that the power of Christ may dwell in me. Therefore, I delight in weaknesses, in insults, in distresses, in persecutions, in difficulties, on behalf of Christ; for when I am weak, then I am strong. "(2 Corinthians 12:7–10). The struggle which Paul experienced was not for a short time and his prayer was not only three times but a prolonged time of prayers over at least fourteen years that he was afflicted with what he called thorn in the flesh. The potential thorn in the flesh referred to by Paul could be weaknesses, hardships, calamities, hardships, and insults. The thorn in the flesh could, also, be any difficulty which humans face. The thorn in the flesh comes in many different formats. The 'thorn in the flesh' could be considered as another word for battle, therefore, whatever battle humans are fighting is their thorn in the flesh. The use of three in the Bible indicates a continuous process. Therefore, when Paul indicated that he prayed three times for the thorn in his flesh to be removed, he was saying that he prayed ceaselessly for many years. At a point he came to the realization that what was important for him, regardless of his problems, was the strength that was from God. He realized that the grace from God outweighs his battle, the thorn in the flesh. The grace which Paul invoked here is an indication that whatever he got from God was not because of his merit, it was because of the love of God to him. He realized that when he was weak, the strength of God could sustain and strengthen him to fight his battle. The grace of God directs DeVine power of God towards him. He was confident that his weakness propelled God to action on his behalf. At that point of an eye opener of God's strength in his weakness, the power of God was manifested, and he became excited and appeared to be relishing his condition of weakness. The only part Paul played in fighting his battles was the contribution of his weakness. Although that was not a valuable contribution by human standard, but God appreciated Paul's contribution. This is because human weakness and submission attracts God to action, and it does not repel God. Human strength is not where God's power lies, but God's power and grace lie in human weakness and frailty. Paul was elated about his weakness because he realized that his weakness qualified and opened him to receive strength and blessing from God. The ingredients to receiving continuous divine power from God are embedded in human weakness, failure, inability, smallness, the past, and in adequacy. Therefore, humans need to realize that it is better to experience valleys with God than to experience mountain top experience without Him, but with the devil.

"Worth Fighting For"

You met me deep in my despair to show me
You would never leave me there
You claimed 'cause I was made for so much more
I am your child
And I'm worth fighting for

Dr. David Ajeigbe

Though heavy with the weight of my mistakes
You carried me and refused to let me sink under the pressure
You meant for me to soar
I am Your child
And I'm worth fighting for
Eyes haven't seen
Ears haven't heard
All You have planned for me
And nothing can separate me from Your love
When there's so much more
Still worth fighting for
Now I'm moving
By faith and not by sight
Towards victory
By the power of Your might
You're straightening out my past
And opening every door
I am Your child
And I'm worth fighting for
Eyes haven't seen
Ears haven't heard
All You have planned for me
(And nothing, no, nothing)
And nothing can separate (can separate) me from Your love
When there's so much more
Still worth fighting for
Eyes haven't seen
(Ears haven't heard) Ears haven't heard
(All You have planned for me) All You have planned for me
(And nothing)
And nothing can separate (can separate) me from Your love
When there's so much more
 Still worth fighting for
That's why I'm pressing (It's worth it)
Towards the mark (So worth it)
'Cause the calling on my life
Is worth fighting for
And I'll keep my mind (It's worth it)
Stayed on You Jesus (So worth it)
Because the peace it brings

Is worth fighting for
And I'll be faithful (It's worth it)
To my wife and children (So worth it)
Because my family
Is worth fighting for
No this world (It's worth it)
Is not my home (So worth it)
But Your kingdom here
Is worth fighting for
I got a mansion (It's worth it)
Over in glory (So worth it)
And my new home
Is worth fighting for
'Til I see it I'll shout (It's worth it)
Hallelujah (So worth it)
Hallelujah, life with you
Is worth fighting for
Eyes haven't seen (Eyes haven't seen)
Ears haven't heard (Ears haven't heard)
There is so much more
Still worth fighting for
Eyes haven't seen (Eyes haven't seen)
Ears haven't heard (Ears haven't heard)
There is so much more
Still worth fighting for, hey, hey
If you believe that you're worth fighting for
Shout to the Lord (There is so much more)
(Still worth fighting for)."
(Brian Wilson/Aaron linsey).

Humans at times go through valleys in life which are not of their own making. In those occasions God might have allowed those valleys to occur. Those valleys might be necessary to bring needed changes to human lives. In the case of Paul, his difficulties were not because of any known sin which he committed, (2 Corinthians 12:7). His difficulty happened as a result of his seeing the glory of God. The Lord allowed this difficulty in his life to keep him humble. Joseph, without any fault of his own, went through tremendous hardships in his life, but God got the glory through them. Job was another devout follower of God who went through several difficulties and sufferings, his difficulties and sufferings occurred because of his righteousness. Sometimes humans go through hardships not because they have brought them on themselves, but because God is doing a work in their lives. "So be truly glad. There is wonderful joy ahead, even though you must endure many trials for a little while" (1 Peter 1:6, NLT). The Psalmist wrote, "Even when I walk through the darkest valley, I will not be afraid, for you are close beside me" (Psalm 23:4, NLT). Any human who might not be experiencing any form of battle in their live presently should brace for when those battles might knock on their doors by moving closer to God who could fight their battles. At that time humans are not to be afraid, but to face their battles with boldness through Christ who is their warrior. Even though humans could not see tomorrow and not sure of what would be appearing in the horizon, but one assurance is certain that God will not abandon humans in their hardship. As God's creation, God considers humans to be worth fighting for and He will always fight on the side of humans to give them victory which they are not able to achieve on their own power, it is obvious that God considered/considers humans worth fighting for when he sacrificed the life of His beloved son to renew, redeem, and recover humans from the wilderness of life and sin to which they have wondered and continue to wonder. Humans should not lose heart when things are not going well because they are worth fighting for and God as the warrior is always ready for the battle. In human fear they run and hide, but God their shield and shelter is ever present to have their backs because they are worth fighting for. All that humans need is the assurance and confidence that God is always with them. Although humans feel inadequate there is the assurance that God is adequate and able. Humans are not warriors fit for the battles of life, but God is supreme, adequate, and able. Although humans are fearful and afraid, but God is all powerful and brave.

> "I'm not a warrior, I'm too afraid to lose
> I feel unqualified for what you're callin' me to
> But Lord with your strength, I've got no excuse

'Cause broken people are exactly who you use
So give me faith like Daniel in the lion's den
Give me hope like Moses in the wilderness
Give me a heart like David, Lord be my defense
So I can face my giants with confidence
You took a shepherd boy and made him a King
So I'm gonna trust you and give you everything
I'll be a conqueror 'cause you fight for me
I'll be a champion claiming your victory
So give me faith like Daniel in the lion's den
Give me hope like Moses in the wilderness
Give me a heart like David, Lord be my defense
So I can face my giants with confidence
I'm gonna sing and shout and shake the walls
I won't stop until I see 'em fall
Gonna stand up, step out when you call Jesus, Jesus
I'm gonna sing and shout and shake the walls
I won't stop until I see 'em fall
Gonna stand up, step out when you call Jesus
Give me faith like Daniel in the lion's den
Give me hope like Moses in the wilderness
Give me a heart like David, Lord be my defense
So I can face my giants with confidence, yeah
Give me faith like Daniel in the lion's den
Give me hope like Moses in the wilderness
Give me a heart like David, Lord be my defense
So I can face my giants with confidence.
I'll face my giants with confidence."
(Matthew Armstrong/Chris Rohman/Ethan Hulse/Dustin Loll).

"For His anger is but for a moment, His favor is for a lifetime; weeping may last for the night, but a shout of joy comes in the morning." (Psalm 30:5, NIV). "So be truly glad. There is wonderful joy ahead, even though you must endure many trials for a little while." 1 Peter 1:5, NLT). When humans are going through variety of battles, they should know that God neither forget them nor abandon them in their battles. With that knowledge humans should rejoice because deliverance is at hand. The lyrics of the song below made it plain that when humans feel alone and abandoned by God, they need to know that God will never abandon them in their battles and He will always come to their rescue when they think that all is lost. What God expects of human is to trust Him that His words will always come through when He said that he would never forsake them.

You Are Not Alone

"Another day has gone
I'm still all alone
How could this be?
You're not here with me
You never said goodbye
Someone tell me why
Did you have to go?
And leave my world so cold.
Everyday I sit and ask myself
How did love slip away?
Something whispers in my ear and says.

That you are not alone
I am here with you
Though you're far away
I am here to stay
But you are not alone
I am here with you
Though we're far apart
You're always in my heart
But you are not alone

'Lone, 'lone
Why, 'lone

Just the other night
I thought I heard you cry
Asking me to come
And hold you in my arms
I can hear your prayers

How Do You Fight Your Battle?!!!

Your burdens I will bear
But first I need your hand
Then forever can begin.
Everyday I sit and ask myself
How did love slip away?
Something whispers in my ear and says

That you are not alone
I am here with you
Though you're far away
I am here to stay
But you are not alone
I am here with you
Though we're far apart
You're always in my heart
But you are not alone
Whisper three words and I'll come running
And girl you know that I'll be there
I'll be there.

That you are not alone
I am here with you
Though you're far away
I am here to stay
But you are not alone
I am here with you
Though we're far apart
You're always in my heart

For you are not alone (You are not alone)
For I am here with you (I am here with you)
Though you're far away (Though you're far away)
I am here to stay (You and me)
For you are not alone (You're always in my heart)
For I am here with you
Though we're far apart
You're always in my heart
For you are not alone
Not alone, oh
You are not alone

You are not alone
Say it again
You are not alone
You are not alone
Not alone, not alone.

If you just reach out for me girl
In the morning, in the evening
Not alone, not alone
You and me
Not alone
Oh, together, together.
Gotta stop being alone
Gotta stop being alone."
(Robert S. Kelly).

How disappointing is it if you are trying to help someone with an issue and it appears as if the issue is more concerning to you than it is to the one you are trying to help. It would be more encouraging for you to put more effort into helping that person if the individual shows interest in the assistance you are willing to give. However, if the individual does not show interest, it could be very discouraging to you, and you might withhold your assistance. A story was told of a student who claimed to be a Christian and misunderstood the word of Christ which says 'ask anything in my name and I will do it for you. The student was lazy and did not do due diligence to study well for an approaching examination but was praying for success in the examination. The student took the examination and failed. Jesus showed the example of work and He even referred to His Father as working. There is no laziness or wishful thinking in heaven. God, Jesus, and the heavenly angels all work. The following text has some responsibilities assigned to humans before they could get the things for which they are praying. "Do you not believe that I am in the Father, and the Father is in Me? The words that I say to you I do not speak on My own, but the Father, as He remains in Me, does His works. Believe Me that I am in the Father and the Father is in Me; otherwise believe because of the works themselves. Truly, truly I say to you, the one who believes in Me, the works that I do, he will do also; and greater works than these he will do, because I am going to the Father. And whatever you ask in My name, this I will do, so that the Father may be glorified in the Son. If you ask Me anything in My name, I will do it. If you love Me, you will keep My commandments." (John 14:10–15). The responsibilities Jesus assigned to humans are to believe Him and to do what He has commanded them. In order words if humans do not believe in Jesus and do not obey His commandments, they do not love Him and they might be on their own. They might not get what they ask of Him. If the student aforementioned had studied hard and had prayed to God and has had faith in Him He would have reminded the student, in the examination hall, all the student had studied. The student's prayers might have been answered and the student might have passed the examination. The student's prayers might have been effective. However, because the student did not do his or her own part, his or her faith was dead. God does answer when humans call on Him to fight their battles, but God expects all humans to do their part and He will always do His part. The Lord will take on humans battles as long as humans are willing to believe, love, and obey His commandments. Those are the responsibilities or work assigned to humans in order for their faith to be alive and in order to receive what they ask of God. James declared, "For just as the body without the spirit is dead, so also faith without works is dead." James 2:26). Although works does not save anyone because it is the gift of God. However, when humans have faith in God it should be evident in their work of goodness to others. This is what the message from James implies. Doing good work brings about the glory of God. Praying to God is putting forth an effort. Putting out an effort is work. When humans put forth efforts God blesses those efforts when praying to Him. Prayer could be considered as work because it takes effort to pray in faith to God. Praying is an effort to praise God for what He has done for the individual or what He has done for others.

Dr. David Ajeigbe

Prayers are offered to God to make requests to Him for human needs. When humans are praying to God in faith, they have put forth some efforts, they have exercised some form of work, and their efforts (work) in faith could be blessed by answers from God. Although human efforts are not prerequisites for their prayers being answered but their efforts increase their appreciation of what God does when their requests are fulfilled by God and their battles are worn. Whenever humans receive any gift without much or no effort being put forth, there is the tendency for humans not to appreciate what is received or to give gratitude to the giver of the gift. Answering human requests or prayers is not what humans deserve, it is not by their good work, but it is the gift from God. However, God expects humans to be prepared for what they are asking and for what He is going to do in their lives when they pray to Him with genuine efforts. Humans putting out good efforts (work) is an indication that they are ready for what they are requesting, and that such could be done for them (faith). A person praying to pass an examination which could be considered to be the person's battle. The person must be ready to handle the responsibilities needed to perform on the job for which the individual is praying to pass the examination. Since God knows that person is not ready for the responsibilities needed after the examination and getting a job such prayers might not be answered as requested. God knows that if such person passes the examination without the preparation to do the job as a Christian, that it could bring blemish to the name of the Lord. Therefore, the answer to the individual might be, no, "you are not ready, you need to put forth more effort (work) before the prayers are answered. Paul admonished Timothy to be proficient in spreading the word of God in order not to bring about shame and disgrace on himself and on the word of God. "Be diligent to present yourself approved to God as a workman who does not need to be ashamed, accurately handling the word of truth." (2 Timothy 2:15). The battle could rage on until the individual is well equipped to win the battle. Praying to God without being fully prepared for what one is praying for could be considered as 'tempting' God. The Bible says "You shall not put the LORD your God to the test, as you tested Him at Massah. (Deuteronomy 6:16; Matthew 4:7). God expects humans to be well equipped for their services to Him and to other human beings.

"All Scripture is inspired by God and beneficial for teaching, for rebuke, for correction, for training in righteousness; so that the man or woman of God may be fully capable, equipped for every good work." (2 Timothy 3:15–17). Good works are important because they enable people to see God in the believers' lives, good works bless others and strengthen the body of Christ, good works are indications of human love for God, good works are indications of the saving grace humans receive from God, and good works will eventually bring rewards to humans. God answers prayers in resolving human battles when humans have done their own due diligence in good works. In going to God in prayers and in faith humans should be well prepared, do their own parts, and leave their battles at the foot of the cross for the lord to take them over.

> You've never failed me yet
> Walking around these walls
> I thought by now they'd fall
> But You have never failed me yet
> Waiting for change to come

Dr. David Ajeigbe

Knowing the battle's won
For You have never failed me yet
Your promise still stands
Great is Your faithfulness, faithfulness
I'm still in Your hands
This is my confidence
You've never failed me yet
I know the night won't last
Your word will come to pass
My heart will sing Your praise again
Jesus You're still enough
Keep me within Your love, oh
My heart will sing Your praise again
(Oh, yes, it will)
Your promise still stands
Great is Your faithfulness, faithfulness
I'm still in Your hands
This is my confidence
You've never failed
Your promise still stands
Great is Your faithfulness, faithfulness
I'm still in Your hands
This is my confidence
You've never failed me yet
Never failed me yet
Oh, oh-oh
I've seen You move, You move the mountains
And I believe I'll see You do it again
You made a way, where there was no way
And I believe I'll see You do it again
I've seen You move, You move the mountains
And I believe I'll see You do it again
You made a way, where there was no way
And I believe I'll see You do it again
I've seen You move, You move the mountains
And I believe I'll see You do it again
You made a way, where there was no way
And I believe I'll see You do it again
I'll see You do it again
Your promise still stands

> Great is Your faithfulness, faithfulness
> I'm still in Your hands
> This is my confidence
> You've never failed
> Your promise still stands
> Great is Your faithfulness, faithfulness
> I'm still in Your hands
> This is my confidence
> You've never failed me yet
> Oh, You've never failed me yet
> And I never will forget
> You've never failed me yet And I never will forget
> (Christopher Brown, Mack Brock, Steven Furtick,
> Matthew James Redman).

The song above is an indication that Jesus who has performed miracles in the past is still at work performing miracles today and He will win human battles for them if only they believe and trust Him, who is able. God has never failed humans yet, but He expects humans to believe in His promise and to move to Him in confidence that he is there for them. If humans will only allow their memories and experiences to serve them right, they will realize that God keeps His words, He moved mountains, He created a way where there was none before, and that God fulfils His words and promises if they will move to Him to resolve their life issues. The Bible testifies to it that the words of God will never fail even if heaven and earth should pass, His words will come true. God promises are that He would never neither leave humans alone nor forsake them. "For truly I say to you, until heaven and earth pass away, not the smallest letter or stroke shall pass from the Law until all is accomplished." (Matthew 5:18). "Heaven and earth will pass away, but My words will not pass away." (John 21:33). God promises to be with humans are revealed in the following verses: "Have I not commanded you? Be strong and courageous! Do not be terrified nor dismayed, for the LORD your God is with you wherever you go." (Joshua 1:9). "Do not fear, for I am with you. Do not be afraid, for I am your God. I will strengthen you; I will also help you, I will also uphold you with My righteous right hand." (Isaiah 41:10).

"Be strong and courageous, do not be afraid or in dread of them, for the LORD your God is the One who is going with you. He will not desert you or abandon you." (Deuteronomy 31:6). There is nothing too difficult for God to do. Whenever human efforts are lacking God steps in, not only to help, but to take over and resolve human issues as long as humans get God involved in their troubles and issues and realizing that on their own, they can do nothing, but with the involvement of God everything is possible. Therefore, humans should reliably get God involved in their battles because the battle belongs to the Lord.

"Keep Believing

When I look into your sad eyes
It makes me feel for you
Cause I don't see the light
That was always shining through
Someone broke your heart
And now it's easy to give up
I'm tellin' you it's not the end
It's not the end of love

[Chorus]

Keep believin', baby
Cause everything happens for a reason
Though tonight tears fill your eyes
Don't stop dreamin', girl
I'll be right here to lean on
You're gonna make it through
I want to see you
Keep believin'
Has anybody ever told you
How beautiful you truly are?
How just one smile from you
Can open up any heart?
You deserve that, too

Let somebody lift you up
You gotta know somewhere out there
You're gonna find love, yeah

[Chorus]

Keep believin', just have faith
 I promise the clouds'll break
And someday soon you'll see the sun
And find someone
[Chorus]

Keep believin'
"(Andrew G. Goldmark/Mark Clifford Mueller).

When troubles come in form of battles humans might be discouraged and begin to doubt the presence of God at the time they need Him most. During those times humans need to realize that God is close to them and that He has not abandoned them, although it might seem that way. The situation could be compared to going on a journey before the invention of the Global Positioning System (GPS). It was when one was closer to where one was going that doubts began to creep in and one, at times, wanted to turn around. However, if one endured, one would realize that the destination was closer before doubting began. This is similar regarding fighting life battles, the closer one gets to the end and winning the battle the greater the tendency to give up and allow doubts to win. It is at that time when humans begin to doubt God's presence. However, all that is needed by humans is to endure to the end because the Lord is always at work with humans propping them up. Jesus in talking about the battles awaiting humans at the end of age stated: "But the one who endures to the end, he will be saved. This gospel of the kingdom shall be preached in the whole world as a testimony to all the nations, and then the end will come." (Matthew 24:13–14). Whatever battles humans are going through, they are encouraged to endure and God will lead them to victory as long as they put God first and get Him involve in their battles. "God is our refuge and strength, A very present help in trouble." (Psalm 46:1). The Psalmist confirmed that God is always present to help humans at all times and more especially in times of trouble (battle). This declaration indicates that God never abandon humans. Humans are to keep believing, dreaming, and trusting God for all assistance needed.

> "The LORD is near to the brokenhearted
> And saves those who are crushed in spirit." (Psalm 34:18).

"Just as a father has compassion on his children, So the Lord has compassion on those who fear Him." (Psalm 103:13. "And not only this, but we also celebrate in our tribulations, knowing that tribulation brings about perseverance; and perseverance, proven character; and proven character, hope; and hope does not disappoint, because the love of God has been poured out within our hearts through the Holy Spirit who was given to us." (Romans 5:3–5).

Fires

… I remember how You told me
That life may not be easy
And everything that I need
You've already given me

… I remember how You told me
I can trust You completely
So why am I doubting
When You proved that You'd fight for me?

… You've walked me through fires
Pulled me from flames
If You're in this with me
I won't be afraid

… When the smoke billows higher, oh and higher
And it feels like I can barely breathe

How Do You Fight Your Battle?!!!

I'll walk through these fires
'Cause You're walking with me

… I'm changed by Your mercy
Covered by Your peace
I'm living out the victory
Doesn't mean I won't feel the heat

… You've walked me through fires
Pulled me from flames
If You're in this with me
I won't be afraid

… When the smoke billows higher, oh and higher
And it feels like I can barely breathe
I'll walk through these fires
'Cause You're walking with me

… I can face anything (anything)
'Cause You're here with me (here with me)
I can do all things (do all things)
'Cause You strengthen me

… I remember how You showed me
The price of my redemption
Lord, how could I question
When You proved that You'd die for me?

… You've walked me through fires
Pulled me from flames (pulled me from flames)
If You're in this with me (thank you, Lord)
I won't be afraid (I won't be afraid)

… When the smoke billows higher (higher)
Oh and higher (higher)
And it feels like I can barely breathe
I'll walk through these fires (I'll walk through)
'Cause You're walking with me

… I'll walk through these fires (I'll walk through)
'Cause You're walking with me
(Jordan St. Cyr/Kristen L. Nordhoff/DarrelKuiper).

The song above should serve as remembrance to humans that God is the giver of every good thing. Every unhappiness which humans feel is not without the knowledge of God. God is aware of those unhappiness, sadness, and disappointments and He stays closely with humans during those difficult times. Although it might appear that God is far, but the opposite is the case because God is always close to the broken hearted. "The Lord is near to the brokenhearted And saves those who are crushed in spirit." (Psalm 34:18). "He heals the brokenhearted And binds up their wounds." (Psalm 147:3). Whenever humans feel broken hearted God is present to heal their hearts. When humans feel that their hearts have been crushed, a look at Jesus will mend their hearts. When humans feel overwhelmed by their battles, a turn to Jesus will win their battles. When humans feel discomfort, God comforts them.

The perception of the future depends on an individuals' experiences, age, and relationship with Christ. For those who have been close and experienced God, their trust in God's providence and sustenance is different from that of those who have not been close to Him. Those who believe and trust God take solace in His ever presence with them. It is very difficult for people of young age and limited life experiences to feel that their battles are not the end of their lives and that they should give themselves opportunities. Some younger people with no past life experiences think that it is the end of the world for them in life. As a result of their lack of experience with battles and how God could see them through the battles, they lose hope and think that it is the end of the world for them. They do not see the options God has provided them to follow and trust Him for their future. With the loss of hope, they might cause their own ends. They do not realize that the present disappointments in their lives could be some blessings in disguise. However, if they move closer to God and trust that He is always going to 'have their backs,' they will be able to see the goodness of the Lord. "I would have despaired unless I had believed that I would see the goodness of the Lord In the land of the living." (Psalm 27:13, NASB1995). Humans are to be encouraged to trust God for His assistance in fighting their battles and not to despair.

Praise You In This Storm

…I was sure by now
God, You would have reached down
And wiped our tears away
Stepped in and saved the day
But once again, I say, "Amen" and it's still raining

…Well, as the thunder rolls
I barely hear Your whisper through the rain
"I'm with you"
And as Your mercy falls
I'll raise my hands and praise the God who gives
And takes away

…And I'll praise You in this storm
And I will lift my hands
For You are who You are

Dr. David Ajeigbe

No matter where I am
And every tear I've cried
You hold in Your hand
You never left my side
And though my heart is torn
I will praise You in this storm

… I remember when
I stumbled in the wind
You heard my cry to You
And raised me up again
But my strength is almost gone
How can I carry on
If I can't find You?

… But as the thunder rolls
I barely hear Your whisper through the rain
"I'm with you"
And as Your mercy falls
I'll raise my hands and praise the God who gives
And takes away

… And I'll praise You in this storm
And I will lift my hands
For You are who You are
No matter where I am
And every tear I've cried
You hold in Your hand
You never left my side
And though my heart is torn
I will praise You in this storm

… I lift my eyes unto the hills
Where does my help come from?
My help comes from the Lord
The maker of Heaven and Earth

… I lift my eyes unto the hills
Where does my help come from?

… And I'll praise You in this storm
And I will lift my hands
For You are who You are
No matter where I am
Every tear I've cried
You hold in Your hand
You never left my side
And though my heart is torn
I will praise You in this storm

And though my heart is torn
I'll praise You in the storm (praise You in the storm)"
(Bernie Hems/John Mark Hall).

Praising God even in the middle of the storm might not change the situation immediately, but it is an ingredient for victory through the hope which God provides to be able to carry on the fight.

One could not raise ones' hands without raising ones' head and looking up to God for help. Looking up to the hills is the confirmation that ones' help comes from the Lord, the Maker of heaven and earth. "I will lift up my eyes to the mountains; From where shall my help come? My help comes from the Lord, Who made heaven and earth." (Psalm 121; 1–2, NASB1995).

When humans raise their hands up and look to the Lord, they are effectively saying, 'My hands are open, I am eager for Your embrace. I am low in the pit; I need Your hands to lift me out. My hands are lifted up and I am waiting for Your hands to be joined to mine. Only by myself I can do nothing, but with Your embrace everything is possible for me; therefore, I surrender all to You. By myself I cannot see the next minute, but You see and have all my life in Your hands. Please, come down to me and fight all my battles.' In fighting their battles and winning, humans need to have total surrender to God's direction and to His leading. Whenever parents return to wherever their children are, either at school, daycare, or anywhere else their children are taking temporary abode or care, the children are always happy to have their parents back to take custody of them. On the first appearance of the parents, the children are very elated to see them and get into their embrace as soon as the environment permits.

Children will run to their parents with their hands raised to the embrace of their parents. What the children are demonstrating is that they are happy to be back in the hands of their parents. The parents are equally happy that they are having their children back in their arms. In like manner, God and the angels with heavenly host are all happy when humans acknowledge God as their defender with all their battles. Children have faith and trust in their parents knowing that their parents are their providers for everything they need and their protector from adversities. This is one of the reasons when Jesus referred in appreciation to the faith of little children. Children are endowed with true faith and true forgiveness. Therefore, Jesus admonished all Christians to be like little children. "At that time the disciples came to Jesus and said, "Who then is greatest in the kingdom of heaven?" And He called a child to Himself and set him among them, and said, "Truly I say to you, unless you change and become like children, you will not enter the kingdom of heaven. So, whoever will humble himself like this child, he is the greatest in the kingdom of heaven." (Matthew 18:1–4). Whenever children get into any form of trouble they run to their parents for protection and to resolve their problems. Children never doubt the ability of their parents to resolve their issues. Children truly rely on their parents to resolve their problems. They never second-guess them. If humans will trust God as little children trust their parents, then the Lord will take over their battles and resolve them. Humans will be at peace in their reliance on God. Although, their battles might not be won as quickly as they expect, they will have the realization that everything happens for a purpose and that God is always in control. Laura Story said it well in the lyrics of her song regarding the reasons some battles might come to humans.

"We pray for peace

Comfort for family, protection while we sleep
We pray for healing, for prosperity
We pray for Your mighty hand to ease our suffering
And all the while, You hear each spoken need
Yet love is way too much to give us lesser things

… 'Cause what if your blessings come through raindrops?
What if Your healing comes through tears?
What if a thousand sleepless nights
Are what it takes to know You're near?
And what if trials of this life are Your mercies in disguise?

How Do You Fight Your Battle?!!!

…We pray for wisdom
Your voice to hear
And we cry in anger when we cannot feel You near
We doubt Your goodness, we doubt Your love
As if every promise from Your Word is not enough
And all the while, You hear each desperate plea
And long that we'd have faith to believe

…'Cause what if your blessings come through raindrops?
What if Your healing comes through tears?
And what if the thousand sleepless nights
Are what it takes to know You're near?
And what if trials of this life are Your mercies in disguise?

…When friends betray us
And when darkness seems to win
We know that pain reminds this heart
That this is not, this is not our home
It's not our home.

…'Cause what if your blessings come through raindrops?
What if Your healing comes through tears?
And what if the thousand sleepless nights
Are what it takes to know You're near?

…What if my greatest disappointments
Or the aching of this life
Is the revealing of a greater thirst this world can't satisfy
And what if trials of this life
The rain, the storms, the hardest nights
Are Your mercies in disguise?"
(Laura Story).

"Goodness of God… I love You, Lord
For Your mercy never fails me
All my days, I've been held in Your hands
From the moment that I wake up
Until I lay my head
Oh, I will sing of the goodness of God
… And all my life You have been faithful
And all my life You have been so, so good

Dr. David Ajeigbe

With every breath that I am able
Oh, I will sing of the goodness of God

… I love Your voice
You have led me through the fire
In the darkest night
You are close like no other
I've known You as a Father
 I've known You as a Friend
And I have lived in the goodness of God (yeah)

… And all my life You have been faithful (oh)
And all my life You have been so, so good
With every breath that I am able
Oh, I will sing of the goodness of God (yeah)

… 'Cause Your goodness is running after
It's running after me
Your goodness is running after
It's running after me
With my life laid down
I'm surrendered now
I give You everything
'Cause Your goodness is running after
It's running after me (oh-oh)

… 'Cause Your goodness is running after
It's running after me
Your goodness is running after
It's running after me
With my life laid down
I'm surrendered now
I give You everything
'Cause Your goodness is running after
It keeps running after me

… And all my life You have been faithful
And all my life You have been so, so good
With every breath that I am able
Oh, I'm gonna sing of the goodness of God
(I'm gonna sing, I'm gonna sing)

… 'Cause all my life You have been faithful
And all my life You have been so, so good
With every breath that I am able
Oh, I'm gonna sing of the goodness of God
Oh, I'm gonna sing of the goodness of God."
(Jason Ingram/Brian Johnson/Ed Cash/Ben Fielding/Jen Johnson).

Conclusion

"Ask, and it will be given to you; seek, and you will find; knock, and it will be opened to you. For everyone who asks receives, and the one who seeks finds, and to the one who knocks it will be opened. Or what person is there among you who, when his son asks for a loaf of bread, will give him a stone? Or if he asks for a fish, he will not give him a snake, will he? So, if you, despite being evil, know how to give good gifts to your children, how much more will your Father who is in heaven give good things to those who ask Him! (Matthew 7:7–11). Jesus gave the assurance that God is always present with humans and provides appropriately for their needs. Jesus gave the assurance to humans that God will always give good things to those who ask Him. In His assurance, Jesus compared humans who are evil to God who is pure. He wanted humans to know that despite their being evil they give good and harmless gifts to their children. God who is merciful and knows the needs of humans will always provide and help humans with any issues pertaining to humans as long as they ask Him and do His will. In His teaching on assurance, He was encouraging humans not to be anxious about anything, but to take everything to God in prayers and God will meet their needs including any battles they are going through.

It is important for humans to know that the Lord will not forget them and to be patient and wait for the Lord for he will fulfil His promises. Micah declared; "But as for me, I will be on the watch for the LORD; I will wait for the God of my salvation. My God will hear me." (Micah 7:7).

There is nothing humans could do on their own power, but they are to rely on the power of God to do for them all that are impossible for them.

> "You are my King, God; Command victories for Jacob. Through You we will push back our adversaries; Through Your name we will trample down those who rise up against us. For I will not trust in my bow, Nor will my sword save me. But You have saved us from our adversaries, And You have put to shame those who hate us. In God we have boasted all day long, And we will give thanks to Your name forever." (Psalm 44:4–8).

The basic meaning of the word boasting is "to praise, " as in the English word "hallelujah, means "praise Jehovah." The Bible encourages humans to engage in proper boasting or praise of other human beings: "Let another praise you, and not your own mouth" (Proverbs 27:2); "a woman who fears the Lord is to be praised" (Proverbs 1:30). "Seek ye the LORD while He may be found, call ye upon Him while He is near: Let the wicked forsake his way, and the unrighteous man his thoughts: and let him return unto the LORD, and He will have mercy upon him; and to our God, for He will abundantly pardon. For my thoughts are not your thoughts, neither are your ways my ways, saith the LORD. For as the heavens are higher than the earth, so are my ways higher than your ways, and my thoughts than your thoughts." (Isaiah 55:6–9, KJV).

"The fear of the LORD is to hate evil; Pride, arrogance, the evil way, And the perverted mouth, I hate. Advice is mine and sound wisdom; I am understanding, power is mine." (Proverbs 13–14). "Pride *goes* before destruction, And a haughty spirit before stumbling." (Proverbs 16:18).

> "An angry person stirs up strife, And a hot-tempered person abounds in wrongdoing." (Proverbs 29:22).

"A person's pride will bring him low, But a humble spirit will obtain honor." (Proverbs 29:23).

"One who hates disguises *it* with his lips, But he harbors deceit in his heart. When he speaks graciously, do not believe him, Because there are seven abominations in his heart. Though his hatred covers itself with deception, His wickedness will be revealed in the assembly." (Proverbs 26:24–26).

…"for the weapons of our warfare are not of the flesh, but divinely powerful for the destruction of fortresses. We are destroying arguments and all arrogance raised against the knowledge of God, and we are taking every thought captive to the obedience of Christ, and we are ready to punish all disobedience, whenever your obedience is complete." (2 Corinthians 10:4–6).

In human affairs there are always the battles between forgiveness and unforgiveness, but only God could resolve those battles. With human nature, the easiest road to take is the road of unforgiveness because of the seemingly temporary satisfaction that it gives.

Forgiveness has the power to heal embedded in it, but unforgiveness is poison to the soul. Humans struggle with the ability to forgive others. The presence of many Biblical passages confirms the difficulty of thought of forgiving others. The Bible encourages humans to strive to forgive those who have wrongly treated them. The Bible emphasizes forgiveness because forgiving others is a battle for humans to win. However, humans need to look at the benefits they could receive by forgiving others rather than on the bad treatments they have received from the perpetrator(s). humans should be encouraged and allow their hearts to live for the glory humans receive from God through His grace and forgiveness for humans. Humans who do not forgive others spend their time and energy being consumed by unforgiveness which is not beneficia but destroys. Paul admonished all to let; "All bitterness, wrath, anger, clamor, and slander must be removed from you, along with all malice. Be kind to one another, compassionate, forgiving each other, just as God in Christ also has forgiven you. (Ephesians 4:27, 31–32).

When humans engage in unforgiveness they imprison themselves in the past and are trapped in it rather than looking, in hope, to God who could make everything better and Who could heal all wounds. When humans dwell in the past, they may be depriving themselves of the assistance from God to win their battles. However, forgiveness looks away from the anguish of the past and focuses on the future for better things to come. It is the desire of the devil to have humans stuck in the past to keep them from moving forward in the glorious plan God has in store for them. "So, as those who have been chosen of God, holy and beloved, put on a heart of compassion, kindness, humility, gentleness, and *patience*; bearing with one another, and forgiving each other, whoever has a complaint against anyone; just as the Lord forgave you, so must you do also. (Colossians 3:12–14). Forgiveness does not mean forgetiveness, that is to say that the offended could not forget the offense, but it means that the offended should let go of retaliation. After forgiving the offenders, humans should see them as Jesus sees them and accept them as Christ has accepted all sinners. Humans should make all efforts to love other humans just as Jesus loves them regardless of what they have done.

All humans have battles with sin and they should be kind and gentle in handling and dealing with other sinners. Humans should realize that they are not righteous apart from the righteousness of God which He has extended to humans. Just as the Bible states that; "The fool has said in his heart, there is no God. They are corrupt and have committed abominable injustice; There is no one who does good. God has looked down from heaven upon the sons of mankind to see if there is anyone who understands, who seeks after God. Every one of them has turned aside; together they have become corrupt; there is no one who does good, not even one." (Psalm 53:1–3). Humans can only win the battle of sin through grace and forgiveness from God. Therefore, humans should not judge another's entire being by one event, but should extend grace to them as they have received from the Lord. Humans are to replicate similar kindness as Jesus has extended to them to be able to win their battles. "... bearing with one another, and forgiving each other, whoever has a complaint against anyone; just as the Lord forgave you, so must you do also. "(Colossians 3:13). "...and he said, Listen, all you of Judah and the inhabitants of Jerusalem, and King Jehoshaphat: "... This is what the Lord says to you: 'Do not fear or be dismayed because of this great multitude, for the battle is not yours but God's." (2 Chronicles 20:15). "The righteous cry out, and the Lord hears and rescues them from all their troubles" (Psalm 34:17). "Oh give us help against the enemy, for rescue by man is worthless. Through God we will do valiantly, and it is He who will trample down our enemies." (Psalm 60:11–12). The Bible gives humans the assurance to go to Him without being afraid of whatever issues they face because the Lord, their God, will give them victories over all their adversaries and battles. All that humans need to do is to put all their trust in Him and He will fight and win their battles successfully.

Note: All Scripture, unless otherwise stated, is taken from the New American Standard Bible version of the Holy Bible.

www.ingramcontent.com/pod-product-compliance
Lightning Source LLC
Chambersburg PA
CBHW052030030426
42337CB00027B/4940